RECIPES
FROM THE
FRENCH WINE HARVEST

Revised Edition

Rosi Hanson
Photographs by Katerina Kalogeraki

First published 1995
by Cassell

That edition created and produced by
Rosemary Wilkinson Publishing

Copyright © Rosi Hanson 1995 & 2015 for the text
Copyright © Katerina Kalogeraki 2015 for photographs

British Library Cataloguing-in-Publication Data

A catalogue record for this book is available from the British Library

All rights reserved. No part of this book may be reproduced, stored, or transmitted by any means—whether auditory, graphic, mechanical, or electronic—without written permission of both publisher and author, except in the case of brief excerpts used in critical articles and reviews. Unauthorized reproduction of any part of this work is illegal and is punishable by law.

ISBN: 978-1-4834-2923-6 (sc)
ISBN: 978-1-4834-2924-3 (e)

Because of the dynamic nature of the Internet, any web addresses or links contained in this book may have changed since publication and may no longer be valid. The views expressed in this work are solely those of the author and do not necessarily reflect the views of the publisher, and the publisher hereby disclaims any responsibility for them.

Lulu Publishing Services rev. date: 07/07/2015

For Anthony and Christopher, with love

TABLE OF CONTENTS

BURGUNDY 1

Grated Carrot Salad with Mustard Vinaigrette 11
Chicory Salad with Mustard Vinaigrette 12
Celeriac with Mustard & Lemon Vinaigrette 13
Green Salad with warm Chicken Livers, Croutons, Gruyère and Tomatoes 13
Cabbage and Apple Salad with Herbs and Crème Fraîche 14
Potted Cheese 15
Poached Eggs in a Red Wine Sauce with Bacon and Garlic Croutons 16
Mme Lafarge's Pot-Au-Feu 18
Meat Pie to use up Beef with Bacon and Onions in a Cream Sauce 21
Stuffed Tomatoes 24
Monsieur Bernard's Stuffed Potatoes 25
Fresh Tomato Sauce 26
A Burgundian Potato Dish with Fresh Curd Cheese and Cream 27
Bernadette Raveneau's Recipe for Gratin of Potatoes and Gruyère 28
Ham in White Wine, Tomato & Cream Sauce with Tarragon 29
Turkey Breasts in a Cream Sauce with Mushrooms and Shallots 30
Classic Burgundian Chicken in Red Wine Sauce with Bacon and Mushrooms 31
Rabbit Cooked in White Wine with Fresh Herbs, Tomatoes and Mushrooms 32
Slow Cooked Beef in Red Wine with Bacon, Little Onions and Garlic Croutons 33
Sauted Pork with White Wine and Sherry Vinegar 35
Bernadette Raveneau's Courgette Cheese Gratin 36
Light Sponge Cake with Fresh Berry Coulis 37
Marie-Thérèse Meurgey's Quick & Delicious Baked Apples 38
Noëlle Lafarge's Fail-Safe Apple Cake 39
Sponge Roll with Home-made Jam 40

RHÔNE 42

Provençale Garlic Mayonnaise 49
Potato and Parsley Omelette to Serve Cold 51
Gratin of Haricot Beans 52
Chickpea Salad 53
Macaroni Cheese the French Way 54
Marie-Pierre Teisserenc's Leg of Lamb Slow Cooked in Red Wine with Figs, Walnuts and Grapes 55
Mme Peyraud's Paëlla with Fish, Chicken and Rabbit 56
Slow Cooked Provençale Beef 58
Leg of Pork or Wild Boar Marinaded in Red Wine 60
Shoulder of Lamb Cooked in Red Wine with Garlic & Herbs, with Dried Haricot Beans 62
Sweet Crisp Fritters 64
Apricot Tart Sprinkled with Muscat Beaumes De Venise 65

BORDEAUX ... 67

Ch. Lynch-Bages' Rabbit with a Stuffing of Pork, Parsley & Garlic ... 77
Roast Guinea-Fowl with Figs in a Cream Sauce ... 78
Veal Stew with Onions and Mushrooms in a Cream & Egg Sauce ... 79
Chicken with Rice and a Cream Sauce ... 81
Poached Stuffed Chicken ... 82
Bacon Joint Poached with Vegetables ... 84
Bacon Joint with Lentils ... 85
French Cottage Pie ... 85
Figs in Red Wine ... 86
Peaches in Red Wine ... 87
Peaches and Prunes Simmered in Spiced Wine ... 87
Simple Apple Compôte ... 88
Little Custard Pots ... 89
Hot Spiced Wine ... 90

LOIRE ... 91

The Biotteau's Onion Soup ... 97
Spinach, Cream & Cheese Tart ... 98
Gratin of Hard-Boiled Eggs ... 99
Potted Pork ... 100
Mme Laroche's Pork Terrine ... 102
Butter and Shallot Sauce from the Loire ... 103
Salad of Potatoes and Smoked Herring Fillets ... 104
Boulettes De Porc From the Sechers' Kitchen ... 105
Roast Pork with Tomatoes, Onions and Potatoes ... 106
Roast Pork in Puff Pastry with Garlic Cloves ... 107
Roast Guinea-Fowl with Autumn Fruit ... 108
Guinea-Fowl with Baked Apples and Chestnuts ... 109
Rustic Duck Stew with Shallots and Potatoes ... 110
Chicken Cooked in Wine with Onions, Mushrooms and Cream ... 111
Sauté of Rabbit in a Mustard and Cream Sauce ... 112
One Pot Rabbit Cooked in White Wine with Mushrooms and Potatoes ... 113
Poached Ox Tongue with Madeira Sauce ... 114
Mme Cotat's Caramelised Rhubarb Cake ... 116
White Wine Cake ... 117
Marinated Pears in Puff Pastry Pie ... 118
Very Fast Salad of Grapes and Apples in Sweet White Wine ... 119

CHAMPAGNE 120

Five Vegetable Soup 126
Potée Champenoise 127
Cabbage and Bacon to Serve with Pork Chops or Sausages 129
Salad of Green Leaves and Potatoes with Hot Bacon 130
Salad of Hot Potatoes, Leaves, Bacon and Onions 131
Rice Salad with Tuna 131
Rabbit Cooked in Champagne 132
Parcels of Veal Escalopes Filled with Pork and Herbs 133
Beef Braised in Red Wine with Carrots 134
Beef Miroton 136
Quick Tart of Apples or Pears 136

ALSACE 138

Casserole of Red Cabbage & Apples 144
Traditional Pickled Cabbage with Smoked Pork and Sausages 145
Pink Purée 147
Chicken Poached in Riesling with Cream Sauce 147
Alsace Noodles 148
French Hot-Pot – A Casserole of Slow Cooked Beef, Pork and Lamb and Potatoes 150
Useful Yeast Pastry for Tarts in the Alsace Manner 151
Plum Tart 152

INTRODUCTION

PICKING THE GRAPES

Everywhere the smell of wine in the making, and underfoot in little towns and villages a mess of discarded stalks and grape-skins – it is the wine harvest! All over France, from the Rhone valley in the south, to the northern vineyards of Alsace, when the grapes are ripe people are busy in the vines, vat-houses and harvest kitchens. The scenery is lovely, the mood lively. Behind the names and vintages of great wines revered around the world are real people, working in the heat or the cold, suffering from blisters and backache, and the odd hangover, meeting up with old friends, making new ones, determined to get the most out of their two weeks escape from routine. They come from all walks of life, taking their annual holiday to pick grapes. Professors work alongside train-drivers, ski instructors with bands of itinerant gypsies; foreign students come to earn some money and get a taste of French culture they never forget. Far-flung members of the vineyard-owning families come home to help.

FEEDING THE PICKERS

Holding it all together, creating the ambiance, are the cooks. This is their story – their skill and resourcefulness and great good humour – as well as their recipes. Their day usually starts at 6 am, and does not finish until 10.00 pm or later. When they finally fall into bed, they are likely to be kept awake by partying pickers. Their work in the kitchen will frequently be interrupted. Perhaps a young picker has gashed a finger as he or she clips bunches of grapes with the secateurs and needs to go to the doctor for stitches. They are regularly called upon to minister to pickers suffering from sunstroke, or gastric problems, or to sort out the language difficulties of any foreign students, not to mention acting as agony aunts to the lovesick. Often they have the responsibility of keeping account of who has worked what hours, paying them accordingly at the end of each week. Tiresome paperwork needs to be dealt with. It is they who keep up the morale among the wine-makers, cosseting the cavistes with cakes when, anxious as the mother of a newborn baby, they tear themselves away from the vat-house for late-night snacks. Feeding the harvesters is a tour de force lasting a few weeks, but the recipes are ones we can all use. Very few of the cooks are professionals: usually they are the mothers, wives or sisters of the growers, helped by friends or vineyards employees. Most of them keep notes of menus, recipes, quantities and cost, from harvest to harvest, handing them on to the next generation as it takes over.

SOCIAL HISTORY

At quiet times of the year I have sat at the kitchen tables of many of these cooks, delving into dog-eared notebooks which one day will be an important social record as the traditions of rural life are eroded. They record how they stick to a strict budget, using seasonal ingredients to make traditional old favourites; they show how to turn leftovers into delicious meals. Filled with details of who was there and what the weather was like during the vintage, with photographs stuck in from time to time, and reminders to "use the big black casserole for this", they bring the wine harvest richly to life. In some villages these traditions are dying. When the vintage has been mechanised, no pickers are needed nor do regional dishes always survive when growers employ outside caterers. But these are eminently practical and delicious country recipes - tested by generations of wine-makers' families - which migrate smoothly to town kitchens and modern lifestyles, where I hope they will take on a new life.
ROSI HANSON 1995

Now, in 2015, it seems to me even more important to record these harvest traditions. Amongst the smaller domaines more members of the extended family have full time careers that do not permit them to man the stoves during the vintage. Paperwork has become increasingly onerous, as legislation protecting the rights of temporary workers is more stringent. Some growers fear that it will not be long before the dormitories and washing facilities they provide are inspected, measured and declared unfit, despite the fact that generations of pickers have happily used them. Few would have the money or will to rebuild to current specifications. Some of the families I visited have changed the way they feed their pickers for the reasons above. In others, one generation has handed on to the next but much has stayed the same. In a few cases, the vineyards have changed hands. This revised edition contains most of the recipes I originally collected, with some corrections. The photographs are new. It remains a great celebration of French rustic food from the vineyards.
ROSI HANSON 2015

BURGUNDY

Burgundy is a large region composed of four départements, the Yonne, the Nièvre, the Côte d'Or and Saône et Loire but when wine lovers say 'Burgundy' they often mean the 'Côte d'Or' - the golden slope. Elsewhere in Burgundy a great deal of good wine is made, notably in Beaujolais and Mâconnais, and, increasingly good value, on the Côte Chalonnaise and around Mercurey, but it is the Côte d'Or which is most prestigious in terms of world renown. The Côte d'Or is divided in two halves, known as the Côte de Beaune and the Côte de Nuits. Geographically it is astonishingly small. As you drive along the N74 from Dijon to Chagny, on one side of the road is a band of perfectly oriented vineyards on limestone soil, on the other the plain, where the few vines that are planted produce an everyday-drinking wine, and you are more likely to see other crops. Passing the villages on the 'right' side of the road is like reading one of the world's most expensive wine-lists; names like Gevrey-Chambertin, Chambolle-Musigny, Vosne-Romanée, Nuits-St Georges, Aloxe-Corton, Beaune, Pommard and Meursault are just a selection.

Rosi Hanson

Many of these villages have taken the name of their best Grand Cru vineyard - for example, the village of Gevrey added Chambertin, the name of its most famous Grand Cru (thus confusing consumers all over the world who may pay a lot for a bottle of Gevrey-Chambertin, thinking they are getting Le Chambertin).

The wine labels of Burgundy are notoriously complicated. The easiest way to understand the different levels of quality is to visualise a pyramid. Start at the base: the bottom half of the pyramid is made up of regional wines - on the label it will say Beaujolais, or Mâcon Blanc, or Bourgogne Rouge, for example. Going up the steps of the pyramid, in terms of quality, next come wines from an individual village, like Pommard, or Chambolle-Musigny. Within each village a band of vineyards has been classified First Growths (Premier Crus). On their labels they are allowed to put, first the village name, then the vineyard in letters of the same size, i.e. Pommard Les Epenots, or Chambolle-Musigny Les Amoureuses. You might think that First Growths were the best wines, that is after all the case in Bordeaux, but not in Burgundy. The greatest vineyards of Burgundy, and now we reach the peak of our pyramid, where the volume produced is tiny, are the Great Growths (Grands Crus), i.e. Le Musigny or Le Corton, Le Chambertin, Le Montrachet, and so on.

All this is further complicated by the fact that, unlike most wine-growing areas, Burgundy's vineyards are split up among many owners. The Great Growth, Clos Vougeot, is a famous example, with its eighty or so owners, each cultivating their rows of vines and vinifying their wine in their own way. Owners of some of the finest estates (domaines) may have rows of vines in a number of the Great Growth or First Growth vineyards of several neighbouring villages.

It is rare for a family to live in a large house or château surrounded by their vines as is the case in Bordeaux. Estates are small: a typical estate supporting a family might be just ten to fifteen acres. Land changes hands rarely and then for astronomical prices. Wine-making remains essentially a family business, with sons and daughters taking over from their parents in gradual succession.

There are two grape varieties producing the finest wines: Pinot Noir for the reds and Chardonnay for the whites. The white Aligoté grape produces a lighter, fresher wine mainly drunk locally and the Gamay is planted throughout the Beaujolais, giving a youthful, fruity, red wine. In Chablis, in northern Burgundy, is another pocket of expensive and sought-after white wines. The grape is again the Chardonnay.

The beautiful town of Beaune is the undisputed capital of Burgundy's wine marketing, and one of the most visited of all France's historic sites. Layers of history, from prehistoric to Roman to Renaissance, make this a fascinating architectural study quite apart from the town's long connection with wine. (There is a museum of wine, the Musée du Vin.) The old walls are partly intact and at the centre is the jewel in historic Beaune's crown, the Hospices de Beaune, founded in 1443 by Nicholas Rolin for the benefit of the poor and the sick, with its spectacular and much photographed, coloured, tiled roof. On the way to the flourishing Saturday market, glimpses of these tiles are a special pleasure.

Equally spectacular is the auction which is held each year of the Hospices' wines. Over the centuries the charity has been endowed with an impressive estate of vineyards, the wines from which are sold each November. This event is the centrepiece of 'Les Trois Glorieuses', which draws crowds, including buyers from all over the world, to enjoy a jamboree of banquets, tastings and wine-gossip.

Rosi Hanson

FEEDING THE PICKERS

Picking machines are hardly ever seen in the Côte d'Or and pickers often come from far afield, returning year after year to the same estates. Food plays a large part in this fidelity, with pickers requesting their favourite dishes every year, dishes like pot-au-feu or crapaudine, a Burgundian dish in which layers of sliced potatoes, pork fat and grated Gruyère cheese are baked slowly in a large cast-iron casserole. Perhaps they like these old-fashioned recipes not only because they are sustaining but also because they are the real cuisine familiale, or home cooking, which few people are lucky enough to eat these days.

Around the end of May, beginning of June, winemakers are afflicted with the kind of restless anxiety usually found in women awaiting the birth of a child. They are waiting for the flowering of the vines. It is crucial. Will it pass smoothly? Or will a year's work be ruined by strong winds, violent rain or even hail? If all goes well and they can walk among their vines inhaling the faint, sweet smell of the little white flowers, they can heave a sigh of relief and start calculating, roughly at least, the dates of the harvest. At this moment many growers' wives are already thinking about how they will feed the harvesters.

HARVEST HEROINES

The harvest cook has to think ahead to the time when she transforms herself into a restaurant manager and chef rolled into one. The trick is l'intendance, being organised, having a plan of campaign. Many grow their own vegetables and fruit so, earlier in the year, the cook makes sure enough potatoes are sown and that there will be enough herbs and salad in the garden for when they are needed. She grows plenty of tomatoes, peeling and bottling some, preparing and freezing others ready for pizzas. The biggest of the crop will end up on the harvest menu as tomates farcies, so they are frozen, as soon as they ripen, the insides having been scooped out to be used in soups and sauces. As they come into season she bottles or freezes haricots verts and makes jam from soft fruit to use for the harvesters' breakfast. Many harvest cooks make and preserve terrines and pâtés which come in handy for evening meals. These usually start with soup, followed by cold meats, a hot vegetable dish, green salad, cheese and a simple dessert like a fruit compôte, unless a picker's birthday or a saint's day is being celebrated: this calls for a dessert elabouré - a gâteau roulé perhaps for which that homemade jam is useful, or a gâteau aux pommes.

The final preparations take about ten days. Many wine-makers have a house, shut up most of the year, where pickers are lodged. Usually simple, shabby almost, with lino on the floor and only the bare essentials, it will be scrubbed and cleaned until it is spotless.

The cook will have consulted her notebook with its lists of menus and quantities from previous years and prepared her shopping lists, working always two or three days in advance for basic supplies.

Once the harvest begins, the cook's day starts at about 5.30 a.m. when she prepares breakfast. At 6.15 she may go up the road to the baker for the fresh baguettes. At 6.30 she wakes the pickers - the whole thing is timed like a military operation. Breakfast, usually consisting of a choice of tea, coffee or hot chocolate, cereals with milk, perhaps collected from a nearby farm, then fresh bread and butter and jams, is served from 6.45 until the trucks arrive at 7.15 to take the picking team to the vines.

By the the time she has cleared the refectory - a rather grand name for the simple rooms with concrete floors and trestle tables that are the norm - the cook is more than glad to sit down in peace to her own breakfast and spend half an hour thinking and planning the day.

In the vines work starts promptly. The foreman deploys his workers, handing out secateurs and paniers and allotting rows to those who will cut the grapes. Bigger containers are given to the hotteurs whose job it is to hop over the lines of vines collecting the grapes from the pickers, and empty them onto the trucks waiting to take them to the vat-house. In the early morning mist voices are muffled; the pickers soon have arms soaked in dew, as they part the leaves looking for the bunches of grapes; later blisters will start, aggravated by the sweet grape juice which makes hands sticky, and backs start to ache from bending over the vines. Gathering the harvest is hard work and food-breaks keep the pickers going. The first, a second breakfast in the vines, is particularly welcome to warm everyone up.

In the kitchen the cook and her helpers start early on the lunch, which often features traditional dishes needing long, slow simmering. Although sometimes eaten outside in the vines, lunch is a substantial meal and certainly not a picnic. The main dish is usually preceded by a salad and followed by cheese, fruit or yogurt. Preparations for the lunch are interrupted while they pack the second breakfast or casse-croûte into a van to go to the vineyard at about 8.30 or 9.00.

After lunch at mid-day the picking starts again at 1.30 and continues until 5.30, when the exhausted team is brought back, eager for a cold drink, a snack, a wash and a rest. There is only a short rest, however, for the kitchen team between clearing up lunch and preparing dinner. Restored by the evening meal, the pickers are usually in party mood but, as soon as dinner is cleared and the kitchen left clean for the next day, the cooks are ready to fall into bed.

This onerous schedule is still embraced by many Burgundians, but traditions are dying. Each year fewer estates lodge their pickers, preferring to use local people who go home in the evening. Wives of the younger generation of growers are not always able to take on the cooking if they have full-time careers of their own. Someone who is well-placed to watch this evolving pattern is Marie-Thérèse Meurgey, wife of a wine-broker and for twenty years Adjoint-Maire (Deputy Mayor) of Beaune. Her face lights up when we talk about harvest meals and she begins to reminisce about her own childhood in the Mâconnais, recommending fromage fort (literally, 'strong cheese', a kind of cheese paste) - 'this was something often made for the harvest - it is wonderful!'

What follows are the stories and recipes of some of those wine-makers who, still, as Marie-Thérèse says, really make the harvest into a celebration.

PAIN AU CHOCOLAT IN THE CHABLIS VINEYARDS

Domaine Raveneau's wines are found on the wine lists of the world's most renowned restaurants. To meet a worldwide demand there is only a small amount of wine bearing the great names of the best Chablis vineyards so they are expensive, but wine writers and wine-lovers agree that Jean-Marie's white wines are the crème de la crème.

At 8.30 in the morning the slopes of Chablis are still enveloped in mist and the pickers are wet and cold. A bundle of dry vine-shoots, the product of earlier pruning, is waiting to make a small bonfire to warm them up during the break for the casse-croûte.

The Raveneau's Deux-Chevaux van bumps its way up the chalky, unsurfaced road to the Grand Cru vineyard called Blanchot, high above the little town which, normally sleepy, has been thrown into action by the harvest. The workers finish their rows as the plastic bottle-carrier of vin rouge and the basket filled with the picnic of crusty baguettes, marinated herrings, salami sausage, Camembert cheese and a big slab of dark chocolate are lifted out of the van and the fire is lit.

Recipes from the French Wine Harvest

The pickers stand around the fire at the edge of the vineyard, stamping their feet, eating and knocking back tumblers of the rough wine. Someone produces an ancient Opinel penknife to hack off the slices of salami. The vinegary raw herring goes down surprisingly well after the early morning start. As they warm up, some of them cross the little road to a grassy bank where they can sit and smoke in the weak sunlight which is beginning to penetrate the mist.

The fire dies down and Jean-Marie Raveneau puts a small grill over the embers. He breaks off a piece of baguette, splits it open and toasts it a little on the grill. Then he makes a sandwich of it with a piece of dark chocolate and puts it back on the fire until the chocolate begins to melt into the bread. 'It's delicious, but you must have it with this.' One of Jean-Marie's cellar-workers has just arrived with the tractor and trailer from the vat-house. He passes round a venerable-looking bottle, ratafia, a wine fortified with marc or brandy; to go with the pain au chocolat.

MADAME LAFARGE'S POT-AU-FEU

On the Côte de Beaune, in Volnay, which is renowned for its red wines, Michel Lafarge is supervising the arrival of the grapes in the cuverie or vat-house. This family makes a range of mainly red wines from Bourgogne Rouge to village Volnay to First Growths like Beaune Grèves and Volnay Clos des Chênes. The streets of the small village are blocked by tracteurs enjambeurs (the special long-legged tractors made to straddle the rows of vines) pulling their loads of grape-filled crates from the vineyards. Now, at mid-day, it is rush-hour as the trucks bring the pickers down from the surrounding slopes.

Madame Lafarge finishes supervising the laying of the table as the harvesters are hosing down their muddy boots. Salads are on the table for the first course; in the kitchen the windows are steamed up as the pot-au-feu simmers. A fresh tomato sauce is being prepared to go with it; the cook is putting the cooked tomatoes and plenty of parsley through a large food-mill.

By the time the pot-au-feu has been cleared and the cheese is on the table, the pickers are relaxed and start singing. 'This group is always singing,' says Noëlle Lafarge, smiling. 'Most of them come from the same village in the Bresse and they all know each other - in fact most of them are related - so the atmosphere is good. One man has been coming for twenty years - we're having a little celebration tonight, but don't say anything because it's a surprise".

Many of the people I spoke to are experts in l'art d'accomoder les restes, that wonderfully French way of economically turning left-overs into something special. Chez Lafarge they use up the left-overs from the pot-au-feu in a pain de viande the following day at supper. It is served as a first course with a tomato sauce, and followed by a herb omelette, green salad, cheese and a dessert of home-bottled cherries in syrup. The pain de viande is made by mincing the cold beef and mixing it with enough egg and cream to make it moist. Chopped onion and parsley are added before putting the mixture into a soufflé dish and baking it in a moderate oven for about 30 minutes. It is unmoulded and served hot with the tomato sauce in a separate sauce-boat or bowl. This economical dish is easy to make and very good.

Other favourite ways of transforming left-over meat are to mince it and use it as a filling for a tourte (top and bottom pie made with short pastry), for stuffing tomatoes, or for hachis Parmentier, the French equivalent of cottage pie. It is a source of pride that everything is put to good use and this can include vegetables as well as meat.

*The much-loved Mme Lafarge died in 2013.

HOME COOKING - LA CUISINE FAMILIALE

No Burgundian harvest is complete without the traditional boeuf bourguignon, says Colette Imbert, who used to cook for the pickers of the Domaine Leflaive and those of the merchant Olivier Leflaive in Puligny Montrachet. The Domaine, which has vines in the Grands Crus of Montrachet, Chevalier-Montrachet, Bâtard-Montrachet and Bienvenues-Bâtard-Montrachet as well as other Puligny vineyards, has been in the Leflaive family for over 250 years.

Sixty or seventy people sit down to lunch together here during the harvest and Mme Imbert has a clear understanding of what is needed. 'The harvest meals are simple but nourishing without being too heavy because the position for cutting the grapes is not particularly favourable for good digestion,' she says. 'La cuisine est donc familiale' (therefore, family dishes are what we serve).

Her lunch menu might be a green salad with hard-boiled eggs, followed by the famous boeuf bourguignon served with garlic croûtons and steamed potatoes or a green salad with chicken livers followed by escalopes de dinde à la crème (escalopes of turkey breast in cream with mushrooms) and the meal would end with cheese and fruit. In the evening, as she says, people can take their time and the meal is more relaxed. A vegetable soup may be followed by a lentil salad and croissants au jambon (a slice of ham rolled up in puff pastry with plenty of grated Gruyère and baked for a few minutes in a hot oven) or by slices of raw country ham and gratin de macaroni and end with cheese and apple tart.

A little further north, on the Côte de Nuits, at the most famous of all these great Burgundian estates, the Domaine de la Romanée-Conti, meals follow a similar pattern. That Managing Director, Aubert de Villaine, is not overweight is something of a miracle for not only is the food excellent here, but equally delicious are the harvest meals at the Bouzeron domaine that he and his Californian wife own. When these two estates' harvests overlap, as they often do, Aubert must find himself hard put to choose between coq au vin in Vosne-Romanée or ragoût de porc à la Bouzeronnaise at home. (He would claim, no doubt, that he is far too busy worrying about the wine-making to think about food).

'It's hard work, but I love the harvest,' says Pamela de Villaine whose menus include versions of traditional French recipes from the American writers Julia Child and Richard Olney as well as dishes such as stuffed potatoes, lapin du Vertempière and desserts evolved by Yves Bernard, a chef who for three years took his annual holiday to coincide with the harvest and cooked for the de Villaine's pickers.

END OF HARVEST MEANS PARTY TIME

Throughout France the last load of grapes of the harvest is celebrated by decorating the tractors with flowers and branches from the vineyards and verges - sometimes gardens are raided to make a good show - and driving in convoy, with horns hooting, lights blazing, back to the vat-house. At the Lafarges' the tradition is that the last grapes are emptied into the fouloir-égrappoir (the machine that de-stalks and crushes the grapes) by the women pickers.

Villages often have their very local customs. In Volnay a church service is held before the harvest begins and growers bring some of their grapes to be blessed.

Above the village among pine trees and commanding a splendid view over the hillside of vines, the roofs of the village and across the plain, is a large statue, the Madonna of the vines. Standing here, Chantal Lafarge points out the vineyard where her husband Frédéric, son of Michel and Noëlle, is supervising the picking. After the harvest the Lafarge family will join other growers from the village, and their families, in climbing the steep path to the Madonna, a little pilgrimage after a Thanksgiving Mass in the church.

Rare is the French wine-grower who does not celebrate the end of the work and thank the team of pickers with a party. This event is known here in Burgundy as la Paulée. The families often invite friends and relations to join them and this copious meal usually includes the best of their repertoire of harvest dishes.

The village of Meursault has turned la Paulée into a rather special communal event. In the 1920s, when Burgundy wines were not selling well, a leading grower, Comte Lafon, suggested that all the growers from the village should get together, with their families and guests, among whom would be potential buyers, for a celebratory lunch. Each family would bring its best bottles to this banquet. So successful has this event become that now buyers and wine connoisseurs from all over the world vie for an invitation. La Paulée de Meursault forms part of the 'Trois Glorieuses' in November when the Hospices de Beaune holds the celebrated auction of its wines. The participants in Meursault's lunch rarely rise from the table, except to go into a cellar to do some tasting, before dusk and sometimes a good deal later.

Recipes from the French Wine Harvest

GRATED CARROT SALAD WITH MUSTARD VINAIGRETTE
Carottes Râpées, Sauce Moutarde

More often than not harvest lunches start with salads such as the ones that follow. For all of these you will find that if you double the quantities, the recipe will serve about 10 people.

FOR 4 PEOPLE
3 or 4 medium carrots
1 tablespoon chopped fresh parsley

FOR THE VINAIGRETTE:
1 tablespoon Dijon mustard
4 tablespoons of groundnut or sunflower oil
1 teaspoon red or white wine vinegar
salt and black pepper

Wash, peel and grate the carrots coarsely. Wash, dry and chop the parsley.

The vinaigrette is made rather like a mayonnaise (in fact it is sometimes called a false mayonnaise). Put the tablespoon of mustard in a small bowl. Slowly, drop by drop at first, add the oil, stirring all the time to incorporate it. It can easily separate, so be cautious. (Despite this it will only take about five minutes to make.) Add the vinegar, a pinch of salt and black pepper.

Optional: a teaspoon of boiling water can be added at the end to stabilise the sauce.
Just before serving mix carrots, parsley and sauce together.

CHICORY SALAD WITH MUSTARD VINAIGRETTE
Salade d'Endives, Sauce Moutarde

It is a confusing fact that what the French call 'endive' we call chicory, and what they call 'chicorée' or 'chicorée frisée' is curly endive to us.

FOR 4 PEOPLE
500g (1 lb), or slightly more, chicory
ingredients as for the vinaigrette above

Remove any old, wilting, outer leaves from the chicory.

Cut off the base. Cut out the inner bitter heart, which means scooping out about 3 cm (1½ in) from the base upwards with a pointed knife. Rinse and dry. Slice them in rounds of about 3-4 cm (1½ in). Now they are ready to mix with the mustard vinaigrette (see carrot salad instructions).

CELERIAC WITH MUSTARD & LEMON VINAIGRETTE
Céleri-Rave Remoulade

This salad is widely available in French charcuteries but is easily made at home and makes an appetising first course.

FOR 4 PEOPLE
1 small celeriac
1 tablespoon fresh parsley
juice of half a lemon
ingredients as before for the
vinaigrette (see grated carrot salad with mustard vinaigrette recipe), replacing the
vinegar with lemon juice

Scrub, peel and grate the celeriac. Some people prefer to cut it into matchsticks. Mix it with a little lemon juice while you make the sauce, or it will go grey. Wash, dry and chop the parsley.

Make the sauce as in the grated carrot salad recipe above. Mix all together and serve.

GREEN SALAD WITH WARM CHICKEN LIVERS, CROUTONS, GRUYÈRE AND TOMATOES
Salade de Foies Blondes

FOR 6 PEOPLE
250 (8 oz) fresh or frozen chicken livers
1 batavia, escarole or frisée salad
250 g (8 oz) tomatoes
125 g (4 oz) Gruyère
1 large slice of white bread
olive or other vegetable oil
red or white wine vinegar
salt and black pepper

If you are using frozen livers, remember to thaw them completely ahead of time.

Wash and dry the salad. Cut the tomatoes in half, scoop out the seeds and discard, cut the flesh in dice. Dice the Gruyère. Put the green leaves, tomatoes and cheese in a bowl big enough to allow you to turn them in the vinaigrette.

Dice the bread and fry in a little oil until browned. Keep warm. Carefully clean the livers, cutting out any green spots and removing any filaments. If they are large, cut them in two or three pieces.

When you are ready to serve the salad, toss the livers in a little oil - about five minutes over a brisk heat should be enough, allowing them to brown on all sides but remain a little pink inside. Add the croûtons and livers to the salad.

Deglaze the hot pan with about a tablespoon of vinegar. Off the heat swirl it round, dislodging any little crunchy bits and the juices from the livers with a wooden spoon. Pour over the salad. Add about three tablespoons of oil to the pan and do the same again. Sprinkle the salad with a little salt, grind some black pepper over it, turn vigorously and serve.

CABBAGE AND APPLE SALAD WITH HERBS AND CRÈME FRAÎCHE
Salade de Choux aux Pommes

When the vintage weather is hot, this salad, crunchy and slightly creamy, is refreshing.

FOR 4 PEOPLE
1 small Dutch or Savoy cabbage
(these are the pale green, tightly packed,
hard cabbages, although the Savoy has beautiful
dark green outer leaves)
the same weight in dessert apples, such as Cox's
2 tablespoons lemon juice
3 tablespoons olive or sunflower oil
1 tablespoon fresh chopped parsley
1 tablespoon fresh chopped chives
salt and black pepper
1 tablespoons crème fraîche

Wash the cabbage. Trim off the outer leaves, stalk and the thickest ribs. Cut into four. Soak for 10 minutes in salted water. Drain and rinse thoroughly, drain again. Slice into fine strips.

Peel the apples or leave the skin on, as preferred, then quarter and core them. Slice thinly.

Mix the lemon juice, oil, salt, black pepper and herbs together. Have the cabbage and apple ready in a bowl and mix thoroughly with this sauce.

At the last minute add the crème fraîche and turn the salad again. Serve straightaway.

Recipes from the French Wine Harvest

POTTED CHEESE
("strong cheese" as described by Marie-Thérèse Meurgey) Le Fromage Fort

"You take some hard goat's milk cheese, or a mixture of goat's and cow's milk cheese, and grate it. I usually put in some Gruyère, finely grated. Pour over a large glass of white wine and a little marc de Bourgogne (or brandy), add some finely chopped garlic and some soft white cheese. Use a fork to mix everything together. Leave in a bowl for 24 hours - put it somewhere cool (not as cold as a fridge as it's going to ferment a little - but not too hot either!). And that's all. You know, this is a wonderfully economic little dish - it's a good way to use up the ends of cheeses, even Camembert."

Approximate quantities: 4 tablespoons hard cow's milk cheese such as Gruyère to 3 tablespoons hard goat's milk cheese (you could use the small cheeses about 5 cm (2 in) in diameter that you see often in France, usually locally made and unnamed or choose a hard cheese such as Cantal mixed with some Tomme de chèvre), to 2 tablespoons fresh white soft cheese.

Marie-Thérèse emphasises that there is no correct version: the recipe accommodates whatever cheese is available and your taste, but the end result should be moist, not liquid - a spreadable paste.

This is rather like the old-fashioned English potted cheese, which was a popular way of using up the end of a Stilton or a truckle of Cheddar.

Rosi Hanson

POACHED EGGS IN A RED WINE SAUCE WITH BACON AND GARLIC CROUTONS
Oeufs en Meurette

Eggs, bacon and toast - the ingredients of an English breakfast, but this could not be more Burgundian. The combination of lardons, onions and red wine is a traditional one here, featuring most famously in boeuf bourguignon and coq au vin.

The mind boggles at the idea of poaching enough eggs for the pickers of any of the larger estates but there are growers who consider this to be a real harvest dish.

In the old-fashioned peasant version the use of onion and of flour is somewhat heavy-handed, and the red wine sauce is left to simmer for about three hours, presumably while the family were out in the vines. When they came home tired and hungry they only needed to poach the eggs before putting their feet up in front of the fire on which they could toast the slices of country bread rubbed with garlic. Methods have evolved to suit modern life-styles.

A note about the wine - naturally this does not call for the most expensive Grand Cru, but do not use anything you would not be happy to drink. A good Bourgogne Pinot Noir would be my choice. It may seem extravagant, but the other ingredients are cheap, and the effect is worth it. Serve the eggs either as a first course followed by something light or as a main course with a salad afterwards.

Recipes from the French Wine Harvest

FOR 6 PEOPLE
6 fresh eggs
1 small onion
1 clove of garlic
bouquet garni (fresh parsley sprigs, thyme, fresh or
dried on the branch, bay leaf, all tied together with a piece of fine string)
½-¾ bottle of red Burgundy
125 g (4 oz) green streaky bacon in a piece
1 tablespoon fresh, finely chopped parsley

FOR THE BEURRE MANIÉ:
1 teaspoon plain flour (for those who avoid wheat flour,
potato flour (fécule) works well)
1 teaspoon butter at room temperature

FOR THE CROUTONS:
1 stick of French bread
1 clove garlic

Take the eggs out of the fridge so that they will be at room temperature when you need them. They should be fresh and not too large, or they will be more difficult to poach.

Peel and roughly chop the onion and one clove of garlic. Wash, dry and tie the herbs in a bunch. Put them with the wine in an enameled saucepan and simmer uncovered for 20 minutes. Make the sure the pan is wide enough to make it easy to poach more than one egg at a time in it.

Meanwhile, prepare the beurre manié by mixing the flour and butter to a paste with a wooden spoon in a bowl. Leave aside, not in the fridge but not on top of the stove.

Cut the bread, one slice per person. Peel and cut the second clove of garlic in half.

Remove the rind from the bacon and cut it into dice to make the lardons. Cook over a high heat until the fat begins to run and they brown, then drain on kitchen paper and put aside until the wine has simmered for 20 minutes. Now add them to the wine, onion, garlic and herbs and simmer for a further 10 minutes. Pour the wine through a sieve into a bowl and return to the pan. From the debris in the sieve, extract the lardons and keep them warm - this is a little fiddly - maybe someone else could be delegated to do this while you poach the eggs. The same useful person could now grill the croûtons, (or they could be baked for about five minutes in a hot oven if that is more convenient), then rub both sides with the cut surface of the garlic.

Break the eggs into a teacup, one by one. Have the wine simmering briskly, but not boiling hard. Swirl the wine round with a wooden spoon. Tip in an egg, then another - two at a time is realistic for most of us. With any luck, the whites swirl round the yolks and about five minutes later you can lift them out with a skimmer, perfectly cooked, onto warmed plates. Timing will vary a bit.

When you have poached the six eggs, take the wine off the heat and quickly whisk in the beurre manié until smooth and shiny. Simmer for about 5 minutes, then pour over the eggs, give everyone some lardons, a garlic croûton and a little chopped parsley.

MME LAFARGE'S POT-AU-FEU

A great dish for feeding a crowd – cheaper cuts of beef slowly poached with vegetables and herbs

As Elizabeth David says in her classic book 'French Provincial Cooking', there is no mystery about making a pot-au-feu. It is one of those French dishes that have arisen out of the necessity to make the best use of economical local ingredients which have then turned into a festive and congenial way to feed a large gathering. These dishes often become imbued with folklore - then people begin to think you can only make them if certain secrets have been handed down through the generations.

Maybe the only mystery is that there is no correct version as far as ingredients go. This is basically boiled meat and vegetables. There is, perhaps, a correct method, or at least, some specific points to be made.

Recipes from the French Wine Harvest

The first is that as the water, with the meat in it, comes to the boil, and it must do this slowly, the grey scum thrown off by the meat must be removed. This means that you must stand over the pot for about 20 minutes with a fine-mesh skimmer, removing scum as it accumulates, until what rises is whitish in colour. This is the only laborious part of the recipe.

The second point is that when the recipe says 'simmer gently' it really does mean very gently - a bubble rising to the surface every few minutes is as fast as it should go - otherwise the meat will cook too quickly and will toughen, and the broth will become cloudy. A piece of meat smaller than about 1.5 kg (3 lb) is really too small to cook in this way. The meat will shrink as it cooks

FOR 6 - 8 PEOPLE
1 marrow bone (if possible)
1.5 kg (3 lb) piece of beef (use one of the cheaper
braising cuts, such as rolled blade or brisket,
although the latter is rather fatty)
6 black peppercorns
2 or 3 turnips, peeled and diced
6 carrots, peeled and diced
6 leeks, sliced
1 stick of celery, sliced, optional
1 onion stuck with 2 cloves
2 garlic cloves
1 bay leaf
6 sprigs parsley
2 sprigs thyme
salt

If you are able to get a marrow bone, have it cut up into manageable lengths, then tie them up in cheesecloth to prevent the marrow escaping. When the time comes to serve the dish, the marrow can be scraped out and spread on bread or toast; it is rich and delicious. If no marrow bones are available, add some beef bones for flavour, removing them at the end. Put the beef joint and the bone into a casserole with cold water (just enough to cover, not too much or you will end up with a watery broth).

Start the cooking gently, gradually bringing the water to the boil. Skim carefully until the scum turns white. Cover the pot and let it simmer gently for at least 3 hours without interruption. About an hour before the end of the cooking, add a few peppercorns, the prepared vegetables, the garlic, the herbs tied up in cheesecloth, and salt to taste.

Serve the meat surrounded by the vegetables, with some of the broth in a separate bowl. A pot-au-feu is usually served with some coarse sea salt, mustard and pickled gherkins, or a fresh tomato sauce, or an aïoli sauce (a thick garlicky mayonnaise, see Rhône section).

A green salad goes well with this dish.

Notes: Another method is to plunge the meat into water that is already boiling hard, to seal the meat. The method given is better if you want the meat to give more flavour to the stock.

If you want to include cabbage, most people advise that it is best cooked separately in some of the broth which you remove from the pot. This is to avoid giving a cabbagy flavour to the rest of the broth which you may want to serve later as a soup.

Some families serve the broth with some of the vegetables in it as a soup course, keeping the meat warm and serving it with the rest of the vegetables and some potatoes afterwards. Others serve all the vegetables and meat together, with a little of the broth to moisten them, reserving most of the broth, to which they may add some pasta or rice, for soup at another meal.

If you are making a pot-au-feu for a relatively small number of people (6 to 8), using a small piece of meat, you may want to increase the number of vegetables, or cook it in a beef stock instead of water. Obviously, making the dish in large quantities intensifies the flavour of the broth.

Recipes from the French Wine Harvest

There are so many excellent ways of using up the meat left over (e.g. pain de viande, hachis Parmentier, tourte, and as stuffings for tomatoes and other vegetables) that it is worth making more than you need for one meal. It is a very economical dish!

In some areas, other meats, such as a piece of mutton, or a boiling fowl, or a good boiling sausage, are cooked with the meat. Everyone is then served with a selection of the meats, accompanied, as described, by the sea salt, pickles and/or sauce, depending on the local tradition.

The three recipes that follow are useful for left-over beef from a pot-au-feu. Harvest cooks often mix it with cold roast beef and/or pork, for example. If they lack meat they top it up with sausage-meat which French butchers make with pure pork, fat and lean, ready minced. Families have their own favourite ways to do them; the following are just a guide.

MEAT PIE TO USE UP BEEF WITH BACON AND ONIONS IN A CREAM SAUCE
Tourte de Viande

FOR 4 PEOPLE
FOR THE SHORTCRUST PASTRY:
250 g (8 oz) plain flour
1 pinch of salt
125 g (4 oz) butter at room temperature
small glass of cold water
1 egg yolk to glaze

Rosi Hanson

FOR THE FILLING:
125g (4 oz) green streaky bacon in a piece
30 g (1 oz) butter
1 medium to large onion
125 g (4 oz) sausagemeat
250 g (8 oz) boiled beef (or other left-overs)
a handful of fresh parsley
salt and black pepper

FOR THE BECHAMEL SAUCE:
30 g (1 oz) butter
30 g (1 oz) plain flour
salt and pepper
250 ml (8 fl oz) milk
nutmeg, optional

To make the pastry, mix the flour and salt in a bowl. Rub the butter into the flour with your fingertips, until it resembles breadcrumbs. Add a little cold water to make a supple dough. Form into a ball and leave in the bowl with a cloth over it to rest for an hour.

To make the filling, remove the rind from the piece of bacon. Cut the bacon in dice to make lardons. Put the butter into a large frying pan and let the bacon cook gently, melting the fat. With a slotted spoon remove the lardons and keep on one side. Peel and chop the onion. Fry it in the bacon fat and butter until it is golden, then add the sausage-meat. Mince, or if you prefer chop, the left-over meat. Add the lardons. Finely chop the parsley. Add these three ingredients to the frying pan. Mix together and stir as the mixture browns. Season with salt and pepper.

For the thick Béchamel, melt the butter in a saucepan. Add the flour, stirring to incorporate it. Gradually add the milk, stirring and letting the mixture thicken as you go. Season with salt and pepper. (Some might like a little grated nutmeg.) Take the mixture of meats off the heat and mix with the Béchamel.

Preheat the oven to gas mark 4, 350°F, 180°C.

Roll out the pastry, keeping back a third of it for the lid. Butter a 20 cm (8 in) pie plate or tart tin. Line it with the pastry, pressing it into the sides and letting it overlap the edges a little. Prick the bottom with a fork. Let it 'seize' in the preheated oven for about 5 minutes.

Fill the pie with the prepared mixture of meats and sauce. Have the pastry lid ready rolled out and cut to size. Cut out a small circle in the centre. Wet the edges of the pastry in the tin. Place the lid on top, and pinch the pastry edges together.

Roll up a small piece of greaseproof paper to form a chimney and insert into the hole in the middle (this stops the underside of the pastry getting soggy from steam). If you feel artistic, cut shapes in any left-over pastry and stick them on with a little water. Whisk a teaspoon of cold water into the egg yolk and brush the lid with it.

Bake for about 25 to 30 minutes, until the top is golden.

Rosi Hanson

STUFFED TOMATOES
Tomates Farcies

This comforting dish is usually served with rice.

FOR 4 PEOPLE
4 large tomatoes
1 thick slice of white bread
a little milk
3 - 4 shallots
1 medium onion
1 clove garlic
60 g (2 oz) butter plus a little extra
250 g (8 oz) left-over meat, minced or chopped
1 large handful of parsley
salt and black pepper
a few dry breadcrumbs, optional

Preheat the oven to gas mark 6, 400°F, 200°C.

Cut off the tops of the tomatoes. Using a teaspoon, scoop out the insides, being careful not to pierce the skins. Keep the pulp and juice to add to the stuffing.

Cut the crusts off the bread. Soak the bread in the milk.

Peel and chop the shallots, onion and garlic. Cook them in the butter until they soften. Add the meat and cook for a few minutes. (If you are using uncooked sausage-meat it will need to cook for longer, till browned.) Add the tomato pulp and juice. Wash, dry and chop the parsley. Squeeze the milk out of the bread (use your hands - it is the only effective way). Add parsley and bread to the mixture and stir well. Season with salt and pepper. Spoon into the tomatoes. Dot the tops with a little butter. Some people like to sprinkle the tops with dry breadcrumbs. Put the stuffed tomatoes in a gratin dish and into the preheated oven for approximately 30 minutes. (Cooking time depends on the variety of tomato and how ripe they are. They should not collapse.)

MONSIEUR BERNARD'S STUFFED POTATOES
Pommes de Terre Farcies Bernardin

This is less well-known than stuffed tomatoes but just as delicious.

FOR 4 PEOPLE
8 medium to large potatoes i.e. 2 per person
1 thick slice of white bread
a little milk
1 large onion
2 cloves of garlic
60 g (2 oz) butter
approximately 250 g (8 oz) left-over meat from a roast, sauté, stew or pot-au-feu (can be a mixture of meats)
1 handful of fresh parsley
a small glass of white wine
a little vegetable oil
salt and black pepper

Preheat the oven to gas mark 4, 350°F, 180°C.

Peel the potatoes. Hollow them out lengthways, using a small spoon, leaving a shell roughly 1 cm (½ in) thick. As you finish each one put it into a bowl of water. (Discard the insides, unless you can use them straightaway for a soup.)

Cut the crusts off the bread and soak in the milk.

Rosi Hanson

Peel and finely chop the onion and garlic. Cook them in butter until soft. Chop the meat and the parsley. Squeeze the milk from the bread. Mix the onions, garlic, meat, parsley and bread in a bowl. Add a little glass of wine and a scant tablespoon of oil, salt and black pepper. Stir well.

Drain the potatoes. Sprinkle the insides with a little salt. Fill them with the stuffing. Oil a baking sheet and arrange the stuffed potatoes on it. Bake for 45 to 50 minutes. Lift them onto a serving dish and serve with a fresh tomato sauce poured round them, or serve the sauce separately.

FRESH TOMATO SAUCE
Sauce Tomate

This sauce goes well with all sorts of dishes, in particular with the stuffed potatoes and the Lafarge's meat loaf.

TO MAKE ABOUT 150 ML (¼ PINT)
1 medium onion
1 clove of garlic
vegetable oil
500 g (1 lb) tomatoes
1 bay leaf
a few sprigs of fresh thyme
a handful of fresh basil leaves
salt and black pepper

Peel and chop the onion and garlic. Cook in a tablespoon of oil until soft. Roughly chop the tomatoes and add to the pan. Add the herbs and simmer, uncovered, for 30 minutes, stirring occasionally. Remove the bay leaf and the sprigs of thyme, and put the rest, if wished for a smooth texture, through a food-mill (mouli-légumes). Taste and season before serving.

A BURGUNDIAN POTATO DISH WITH FRESH CURD CHEESE AND CREAM
Le Treuffé

Le Treuffé is the Burgundian patois for this potato dish. It is usually eaten with a salad as a supper dish or with meat as part of a more elaborate meal.
Use round 'soup potatoes' as the French describe them, not the long waxy ones, which they use for salads.

FOR 6 PEOPLE
500 g (1 lb) potatoes
3 eggs
2 heaped teaspoons plain flour
500 g (1 lb) fresh white cheese, such as Ricotta, or curd cheese
2 tablespoons thick cream or crème fraîche
1-2 tablespoons oil, such as groundnut

The potato and cheese mixture can be made ahead of time ready for the final stage just before the meal:

Wash the potatoes but do not peel them. Cut them up if they are large but it is really better to use smaller ones and cook them whole, so that they do not become watery. Cook in boiling, salted water in their skins. When cooked, drain, and when cool enough to handle, skin them. Take a fork and mash roughly, leaving some chunks - this is not a purée.

Break the eggs into the bowl of potatoes. Sprinkle in the flour, season with salt and pepper. Mix all together. In a separate bowl, break up the white cheese, mashing it with a fork. Add this to the potato mixture with the cream. Mix together without mashing the potatoes too much. It should not be too thick a mixture but neither must it be so liquid that it pours - somewhere between the two.

To cook: Heat the oil in a big frying pan. Tip in the mixture and spread it so it is like a rather thick pancake. Cook for roughly 10 minutes over a fairly hight heat until it is brown and crisp on the bottom. Turn down the heat and continue cooking for about another 15 minutes until the mixture is firm enough to turn over and brown on the other side. The best way to do this seems to be to slide it onto a large plate, invert the pan over the plate and turn them both over. This is quite tricky as the pan is hot but the more often you do it, the easier it becomes.

Cook for another 5 to 10 minutes until the bottom of the potato cake is crisp, then slide onto a warmed plate and serve.

BERNADETTE RAVENEAU'S RECIPE FOR GRATIN OF POTATOES AND GRUYÈRE
Crapaudine

FOR 6 - 8 PEOPLE
1.5 kg (3 lb) firm-fleshed potatoes
(belle de Fontenay type for preference)
500 g (1 lb) salted pork back-fat
500 g (1 lb) grated Gruyère
salt
freshly-ground black pepper

Preheat the oven to gas mark 7, 425°F, 220°C.

Slice the back-fat thinly and use to line a heavy casserole, taking care to cover the bottom and sides completely and reserving some pieces for the top.

Wash, peel, wipe and slice the potatoes, about 0.5 to 1 cm (¼ to ½ in) thick.

Line the bottom of the casserole with the potatoes and sprinkle with Gruyère. Season with salt and pepper. Continue with these two layers, taking care to arrange the slices neatly. Lay the reserved strips of fat on top and start the cooking on the top of the stove - it needs to get really hot.

As soon as the fat at the bottom of the casserole starts to crackle, transfer it to the preheated oven. Continue cooking until the top is golden-brown, then cover the casserole, reduce the heat to about gas mark 2, 300°F, 150°C and continue cooking gently for 2 to 3 hours, lowering the temperature if cooking too fast. It is important to spoon off the fat, which is copious, half-way through the cooking.

The crapaudine can easily be made in large quantities for a party. The amount of fat and cheese used should each be a third of the quantity of the potatoes.

HAM IN WHITE WINE, TOMATO & CREAM SAUCE WITH TARRAGON
Jambon au Chablis

FOR 6 PEOPLE
1 - 2 slices of ham per person

FOR THE SAUCE:
300 ml (½ pint) dry white Chardonnay, originally a Chablis village wine
600 ml (1 pint) well-flavoured chicken stock
500 g (1 lb) fresh tomatoes, diced
6 sprigs tarragon
1 teaspoon tomato purée
salt and freshly ground pepper
300 - 600 ml (½-1 pint) thick cream

Combine the wine, stock, tomatoes and tarragon in a saucepan. Bring to the boil, cover, then simmer gently for 2 to 3 hours.

Strain, then reduce by boiling hard to about one third of the original amount. Leave to cool a little. Stir in the tomato purée. Taste and season. If it is quite acidic, no matter - the cream is going to balance it.

Add the cream to the sauce and simmer while you warm the ham. To do this, arrange the slices in a dish, pour hot water over them and leave for about 5 minutes. Drain off the water, pour over the sauce and serve.

TURKEY BREASTS IN A CREAM SAUCE WITH MUSHROOMS AND SHALLOTS
Escalopes de dinde à la crème

Recipes from the French Wine Harvest

FOR 6 PEOPLE
250 (8 oz) mushrooms
60 g (2 oz) butter
2 - 3 shallots
½ tablespoon sunflower or groundnut oil
6 turkey breast escalopes (if cut by your
butcher they should be quite thin and weigh
about 60 - 90 g (2 - 3 oz) each. If you have to buy the
turkey breast and slice it yourself,
it will not matter if you end up with smaller
pieces - just have more of them)
200 ml (7 fl oz) thick crème fraîche
a squeeze of lemon
salt, pepper and grated nutmeg

Wipe the mushrooms clean and slice thinly. Melt half the butter in a pan and sauté the mushrooms until they are soft and their liquid has almost evaporated. Peel and chop the shallots. Heat the rest of the butter and the oil in a frying pan. When it is hot (but do not let it burn) put in as many escalopes as is convenient at one time without crowding them. When they have browned on both sides, turn the heat down a bit and let them carry on cooking, about another 5 minutes, depending on thickness, until they are cooked through. When they are all cooked, keep them warm on a serving dish.

Sauté the shallots in the same butter. When they are melting, add the créme fraîche, stirring and scraping the bottom of the pan. Let it bubble and cook for a few minutes. Add the mushrooms and seasoning including the lemon juice, tasting until you think it is right. Pour over the escalopes and serve.

CLASSIC BURGUNDIAN CHICKEN IN RED WINE SAUCE WITH BACON AND MUSHROOMS
Coq au Vin

FOR 6 PEOPLE
1 farm chicken weighing about 2 kg (4 lb)
12 little onions or shallots
150 - 200 g (5-7 oz) green streaky
bacon in a pieces
1 tablespoon butter
1 tablespoon sunflower or groundnut oil
salt and black pepper
1 tablespoon plain flour
100 ml (3½ fl oz) marc de Bourgogne or brandy
1 bottle red Burgundy
a bouquet garni of bay leaf, fresh thyme (or thyme

dried on the branch) and parsley
2 cloves garlic
a handful of fresh parsley
250 g (8 oz) button mushrooms, optional
white bread for croutons

Cut up the chicken so that you have two legs, thighs and wings; cut the carcass with the breasts in two lengthways, or, if you prefer, into four pieces.

Peel the onions or shallots. Remove the rind from the bacon and cut into dice, or lardons. Put the butter and oil in a heavy casserole (such as enameled cast-iron) large enough to take the pieces of chicken eventually. Brown the little onions and the lardons. Lift them from the fat and keep on one side. Brown the chicken pieces well on all sides. Season with a little salt and black pepper and sprinkle with the flour, turning the pieces so they are coated.

Warm the glass of marc or brandy in a small pan. Pour over the chicken and immediately put a match to it, standing back so that your eyebrows or hair do not catch fire. When the flames have died down, put back the onions and lardons. Pour in the wine. Add the bouquet garni and garlic. Bring just to the boil, turn the heat right down, cover and simmer very gently for an hour.
Now is the moment to correct the sauce. Lift out the pieces of chicken, onions, lardons, and keep warm. Discard the herbs and garlic. Boil the sauce to reduce it by about a third. Keep an eye on it for about 20 minutes, checking the taste and consistency. (You aim for a consistency that is neither a thick sauce nor a thin stock and a taste which is intense without being over-powering.) Reunite the ingredients, adding the cleaned button mushrooms if you are using them. Simmer for about ten minutes.

While this is happening, slice the bread, remove the crusts and cut into triangles and fry in a little extra butter or oil.

Serve the coq au vin sprinkled with some chopped fresh parsley and with the fried bread triangles arranged round the edge of the dish.

RABBIT COOKED IN WHITE WINE WITH FRESH HERBS, TOMATOES AND MUSHROOMS
Lapin du Vertempière au Vin Blanc

Vertempière is the name of the part of Chagny where the rabbits used by Mme de Villaine are raised. In Burgundy the wine used might be a Bourgogne Aligoté or Bourgogne Blanc, but a Chardonnay from elsewhere could be used.

FOR 6 PEOPLE
1 large farmed rabbit, jointed
olive or other vegetable oil

1 medium onion
1 or 2 carrots
2 large tomatoes, peeled
45-60 g (1½-2 oz) plain flour
½ bottle dry white wine
warm water
2 cloves garlic
bouquet garni of bay leaf, sprigs of
parsley and thyme tied together
fresh tarragon or basil
salt and white pepper
400 g (12 oz) button mushrooms, optional

Brown the pieces of rabbit in a sauté pan in olive or other vegetable oil. While they are browning, peel and chop the onion, carrots and peeled tomatoes into small dice (mirepoix). Add them to the rabbit and let them soften. Sprinkle the flour over the meat to act as a thickener for the sauce. Once the meat is well-coated by the flour, add the dry white wine, stirring and deglazing the bottom of the pan. If the pieces of rabbit are not covered, add a little warm water. As the liquid begins to simmer, add the crushed garlic cloves, bouquet garni, some of the sprigs of either tarragon or basil, salt, and white pepper. Cover and simmer gently for about 45 minutes stirring occasionally.

If you are using them, wipe the mushrooms clean (leave them whole unless they are big) and add them to the pan for the last 10 to 15 minutes.

Lift the pieces of rabbit onto a serving dish. Check the sauce for seasoning. Remove the garlic and bouquet garni and pour over the rabbit. Chop some more fresh tarragon or basil and sprinkle over the top before serving.

SLOW COOKED BEEF IN RED WINE WITH BACON, LITTLE ONIONS AND GARLIC CROUTONS
Bœuf Bourguignon

Mme Imbert always served this during the harvest at the Domaine Leflaive in Puligny Montrachet. No Burgundian harvest would be complete without it! The bourguignon makes a good party dish (quantities for 25 are given at the end of recipe). Mme Imbert served this with steamed potatoes and a big green salad, not forgetting the garlic croûtons, which as she says, makes a 'menu complet'.

FOR 6 PEOPLE
1 kg (2 lb) topside beef
125 g (4 oz) green streaky bacon in a piece
1 large onion
2 cloves

a bouquet garni of fresh thyme, parsley, bay leaf
2 cloves garlic
1 bottle of red Burgundy (Bourgogne Rouge would be suitable)
salt
6 black peppercorns
lard, butter, duck or goose fat for sauté-ing
12 small onions, optional (these are the kind that are used for pickling and not always available; shallots can be a good alternative)

FOR THE BEURRE MANIÉ:
1 teaspoon butter, room temperature
1 teaspoon cornflour

FOR THE GARLIC CROUTONS:
French bread
1 clove garlic, peeled and cut in half

'The most important thing,' says Mme Imbert, 'is to prepare the pieces of beef the previous day, marinading them in red wine (preferably a good one), onions stuck with cloves, thyme, bay leaves, a few garlic cloves, and not forgetting the lardons.'

Cut the meat into cubes about 5 cm (2 in) square, trimming off any gristle or extra fat. (French butchers sell suitable cuts as bourguignon, already prepared.) Remove the rind from the bacon and dice into lardons. Peel the onion and stick the cloves into it. Peel the cloves of garlic and tie the herbs in a bouquet with string. Put everything into a bowl with the wine, salt and black peppercorns.

The next day drain the beef and lardons, keeping the marinade. Dry the meat, including the lardons, carefully before sautéing in the fat. Brown all sides well. This must be done at a high heat - not a thing to do in your best silk shirt - so that the meat cubes are sealed ready for a long slow cooking. Chop the onion from the marinade and brown. If you are using the little onions, peel and brown them whole. Deglaze the pan with a ladleful of the marinade, scraping the bottom of the pan with a wooden spoon to be sure to incorporate the caramelised juices. Add the rest of the marinade with its herbs and garlic. It should just cover the meat - add water if necessary. Bring to the boil. Let it bubble for a few minutes, then turn down the heat, or remove to a slow oven, (aprox. 150 C/ gas mark 2/ 300F) and gently simmer, with the lid on, for about 2 to 2½ hours. It must not go too fast or the meat will be stringy and chewy instead of tender. Test the meat with a fork after 2 hours.

Work the flour into the butter in a bowl for the beurre manié. At the last minute take a small ladleful of the sauce from the casserole and whisk into the beurre manié. When it is incorporated - a matter of seconds - add it all to the sauce and stir it in. Simmer for about 5 minutes until thickened a little.

Cut a slice of French bread per person - grill or bake in the oven - rub with the cut side of the garlic.

QUANTITIES FOR 25 PEOPLE
4 - 5 kg (9 - 10 lb) topside beef
750 g (1½ lb) green streaky bacon in one piece
2 medium onions
3 cloves garlic
3 bottles red Burgundy

Increase the quantity of butter and flour for the beurre manié to dessertspoons. Double the number of peppercorns and use a bigger bunch of herbs.

Increase small onions to 25 if you wish, although when this is done in large quantities they are very often replaced by adding the marinade onions, chopped, and browned at the same time as the meat.

When browning the meat, do not put too much in the casserole at one time as it lowers the temperature of the fat, so that instead of browning, the cubes simply stew, which is not what is wanted at this stage. Better to do a few at a time and keep them on one side until all are browned and sealed and ready to cook in the wine.
If you cook the bourguignon the day before it is needed, you can easily remove any fat that has solidified on the surface.

SAUTED PORK WITH WHITE WINE AND SHERRY VINEGAR
Sauté de Porc au Xérès

At Aubert and Pamela de Villaine's Bouzeron estate this is a favourite dish during the harvest. The sherry vinegar works well with the richness of the pork.

FOR 6 PEOPLE
pork - use leg steaks, one per person, or ask the butcher
for cubed pork for stewing - about 1 kg (2 lb)
1 tablespoon olive oil or sunflower oil
1 medium onion
2 medium carrots
approximately 100 - 125 ml (4-5 fl oz) sherry vinegar
approximately 2 teaspoons plain flour
2 cloves garlic
100 ml (3½ fl oz) dry white wine
100 ml (3½ fl oz) warm water
bouquet garni of bay leaf, sprigs of
parsley and thyme tied together
salt and pepper
fresh parsley for final garnish

If you are using leg steaks cut them into about three pieces.

Brown the pieces of pork in olive oil or sunflower oil in a sauté pan. Brown them well on all sides. Meanwhile, peel the onion and carrots and cut them into dice (mirepoix). Add them to the browned pieces of pork and let them cook in the oil. Once browned add a little of the sherry vinegar to deglaze the bottom of the pan, stirring and dislodging any bits stuck to the bottom. Now add the flour, turning the pork in it so the pieces are coated and the flour begins to brown. Add the crushed clove of garlic, white wine, warm water, bouquet garni, salt and pepper and stir. Bring just to the boil and simmer gently with the lid on for about 90 minutes, stirring from time to time.

Lift out the pieces of pork and put into a clean pan. Strain the sauce through a fine conical sieve over the pork. Taste and add some more vinegar until the balance seems right. Bring just to the boil. Correct the seasoning. Serve the pork in its sauce, sprinkled with chopped fresh parsley.

BERNADETTE RAVENEAU'S COURGETTE CHEESE GRATIN

This is good with a roast chicken but it also makes a delicious vegetable course on its own.

FOR 4 - 6 PEOPLE
(depending on whether served alone or with a meat dish)
500 (1 lb) courgettes (zucchini)
1 tablespoon butter
2 eggs
150 ml (5 fl oz) milk
salt and black pepper
90 g (3 oz) grated cheese (Gruyère, Cheddar or other hard cheese)

Preheat the oven to gas mark 4, 350°F, 180°C.

Butter a gratin dish.

Wash and slice the courgettes. Put them in a saucepan with hardly any water to cover the bottom of the pan (larger courgettes can give off a a lot of water, so take this into account) and a lump of butter. Simmer uncovered until just cooked, 5-10 minutes.

Meanwhile, mix together in a bowl large enough to take the courgettes as well, the eggs, milk, salt, pepper and grated cheese, keeping back a little of the cheese. Add the courgettes to the bowl, stir and tip all into the gratin dish. Smooth the top, sprinkle with the remaining cheese, and bake in the preheated oven until the egg mixture has set and the top browned, 15 to 20 minutes.

LIGHT SPONGE CAKE WITH FRESH BERRY COULIS
Genoise au Coulis de Fruit

Near the de Villaine's vineyards in Bouzeron is a country road where blackberries grow wild. During the harvest, Mme de Villaine picks them to make a coulis to serve with this cake. Some years they ripen too early or too late or other local people get there first, so she substitutes strawberries or raspberries.

You may like to accompany it with a créme Chantilly (sweetened whipped cream). Another way to serve the cake is to cut it in half and fill it with the coulis mixed with some créme Chantilly.

FOR 8 PEOPLE
6 eggs
180 g (6 oz) caster sugar
180 g (6 oz) plain flour
90 g (3 oz) melted, unsalted butter

FOR THE FRUIT COULIS:
250g (8 oz) soft fruit, such as strawberries,
raspberries or blackberries 90-125g (3-4 oz) sugar

Preheat the oven to gas mark 4, 350°F, 180°C.

Butter and flour a loose-bottomed or spring clip 20 cm (8 in) cake tin.

Break the eggs into a bowl. Add the sugar and whisk until white and fluffy and the mixture has doubled in volume. You must beat very thoroughly to get air into the mixture (bear in mind that this cake has no baking powder); using a food mixer saves time.

Have a pan of water ready boiling. Take it off the heat, put the bowl over it and continue to beat until it is warm. Now remove the bowl from the pan and continue to beat as it cools. It will thicken a little and when you can see the traces left by the whisk in the mixture, gently but speedily fold in the flour. Finally, fold in the melted butter. Pour into the prepared tin and bake in the preheated oven for 20 to 30 minutes.

After 20 minutes, test with a pointed knife or skewer - if it comes out cleanly, the cake is ready. If not, continue cooking for a few more minutes before testing again. Cool for a few minutes before turning it out of the tin onto a wire rack.

To make the coulis, wash the fruit and put into a pan with the sugar. Simmer gently. When the fruit has broken down into a purée put it through a mouli-légumes or sieve. Leave to cool.

Pour some of this coulis onto a plate, put the cake on top and sprinkle with icing sugar. Serve more coulis separately.

MARIE-THÉRÈSE MEURGEY'S QUICK & DELICIOUS BAKED APPLES
Pommes Meurgey

This is a nice, homely dish which is even better, says Marie-Thérèse, if you fry the slices of bread or cake a little in butter before preparing the apples.

For each person you need 1 dessert apple and 1 slice of white bread, or sponge cake, or brioche.

Preheat the oven to gas mark 4, 350°F, 180°C. Core the apples but leave them whole. Peel them if you like. If so, you may need to baste with melted butter to prevent them from drying out in the oven.

Butter a gratin dish. Spread the slices of bread or cake with butter and put them in the dish. Arrange the apples, one on top of each slice and bake for about 30 minutes in the preheated oven.

NOËLLE LAFARGE'S FAIL-SAFE APPLE CAKE
Gâteau aux Pommes

Serve this at the end of a meal – it is very popular with the Lafarge pickers.

FOR 8 PEOPLE
180 g (6 oz) sugar
3 eggs,
250g (8 oz) plain flour
3 teaspoons baking powder
1 tablespoon oil (or equivalent of melted butter)
500 g (1 lb) dessert apples

Preheat the oven to gas mark 7, 425°F, 220°C.

Beat the sugar and eggs together until pale. Sieve the flour and baking powder together, then stir into the egg mixture. Lastly, stir in the oil or melted butter.

Peel and core the apples. Cut into chunks. Incorporate them into the batter. Turn into a bottom-lined and greased 25 cm (10 in) cake tin with a removable base and bake in the preheated oven for 30-35 minutes.

Serve warm with crème fraîche.

Pears or apricots can be used instead of apples.

SPONGE ROLL WITH HOME-MADE JAM
Gâteau Roulé

I vividly remember the sight of Bernadette Raveneau running full pelt across the village street separating her own house and the harvest kitchen, carrying this cake hot from her oven. In order to make enough

Recipes from the French Wine Harvest

gâteau roulé for all her pickers to end their supper on a sweet note she was using ovens in both houses. A gâteau roulé cannot wait to be rolled up - it must be done while hot - so she took her life and the Swiss roll tin in her hands (tractors are apt to come round the corner rather fast during the harvest), running to get to the kitchen table where sugared paper and hot jam were waiting. Freshly made and filled with homemade jam, this is certainly worth the run.

MAKES ABOUT 12 SLICES
90 g (3 oz) self-raising flour
3 large eggs
90 g (3 oz) caster sugar plus some extra sugar
3 - 4 tablespoons strawberry, raspberry or other jam

You need a Swiss roll tin measuring 20 x 30 x 1½ cm (8 x 12 x ¾ in) for this. You should line it with parchment baking paper and grease both the tin and the paper.

Preheat the oven to gas mark 7, 425°F, 220°C.

Sift the flour. Take the eggs out of the fridge in good time so that they are at room temperature. Break them into a large bowl. Add the sugar and beat either by hand or using an electric beater. Stop when the mixture is light and fluffy and the whisk leaves a trail when lifted. Now fold in the flour with a metal spoon. Pour the mixture into the tin and smooth the top.

Bake for ten minutes or slightly less - it should be firm when you press it with your finger.

While it is in the oven, gently heat the jam in a pan, so that it is warm and easy to spread.

Have ready a piece of parchment paper the size of the Swiss roll sprinkled with sugar.

Take the tin out of the oven and turn out the cake onto the sugared paper. Spread the jam. Roll up like a long sausage. Your cake is made. Leave to cool. Eat on its own or with ice cream or a fruit compôte.

RHÔNE

Some of the oldest French vineyards are to be found in the Rhône valley. The Phoenicians and the Greeks are thought to have brought their vines with them as they penetrated up the great river Rhône. Later, the Romans established a colony at Marseilles, almost certainly trading wine for slaves.

The towns of Arles, Nîmes, Orange and Avignon with their Roman remains and great markets, full of colour, are irresistible to the traveller. In the warm air of spring and summer the scent of herbs growing wild on the hills is everywhere. The fishing villages and the little, walled, hill villages just behind the coast with their people, food and wines are evocatively described in Sibylle Bedford's autobiographical novel 'Jigsaw'.

In terms of wine, the region splits naturally into two. In the North, from Vienne to Tain l'Hermitage, mainly red wines from the Syrah grape are grown on the steep, terraced slopes overlooking the river Rhône. These are the deep purple-red coloured Côte Rôtie and Hermitage, made to improve with age. The harvesters have tended to come from the nearby villages and towns and often go home for lunch or bring a picnic to eat in the vines. However there are signs that this has changed, following the lead of the Maison Guigal in Ampuis where they take pride in feeding their pickers.

A small amount of delicious white wine is made from the Viognier grape in Condrieu and several other communes along the river, next to the fruit orchards for which this area is famous.

As the Rhône flows south, the valley spreads out into a rich alluvial plain with hills and maquis (scrubland) so typical of this southern landscape. This is a vast production area for red Côtes-du-Rhône and Côtes-du-Rhône Villages from the better placed vineyards. The finest hillside and plâteau sites produce Gigondas, Lirac and, best-known, Châteauneuf-du-Pape.

The spectacular ruin of the summer palace used by the Popes of Avignon after the papal schism of the fourteenth century looks down on the pretty little town of Châteauneuf-du-Pape. The wine of Châteauneauf-du-Pape is traditionally made from 13 different grape types; however, Grenache predominates, (as is the case throughout the Southern Rhône), with Syrah and Mourvèdre of great importance to bring complexity, balance and keeping qualities.

The vineyards are an extraordinary sight because the vines of Châteauneuf-du-Pape appear to grow directly out of a layer of rounded pebbles and rocks smoothed many thousands of years ago on the bed of the Rhône. Somehow their roots find the soil below.

Continuing south, Provence is a useful source of large quantities of rosé and red wines for drinking within a year or two of their harvest. Côtes du Luberon and Côtes du Ventoux are some of the better-known of these wines.

Nearer to the Mediterranean, Rosé de Provence found a ready market amongst the holiday-makers on the Côte d'Azur. The best red and rosé wine here comes from Bandol, where the Mourvèdre grape gives it individuality.

Much of the picking here has traditionally been done by extended families of North African Arabs, or by Portuguese or Spaniards from across the borders, who bring with them their own cooks and their own preferred cuisine. For this reason dishes, such as paella and couscous, (widely available, ready cooked, in the markets of the area) have become associated with end-of-harvest celebrations. Increasingly though, grape-picking machines are being used throughout the Rhône valley, and, as someone there said, it does not take much skill to feed a machine.

SAFFRON AND ROSE - THE COLOURS OF PROVENCE

"When I was a little girl, we used to plant the little corms of the saffron crocus in between the rows of vines. In the autumn we picked the flowers and dried the stamens for fifteen days". Mme Peyraud, an elderly lady elegantly dressed in a pink dress which is slightly paler than the beautiful Bandol rosé wine of Le Domaine Tempier which she poured, was speaking. Brick red when dry, saffron is the essential ingredient in the great fish soups, and the rice dishes of this area, such as paella, staining the broth or the rice a glorious yellow and giving them a very special flavour. The rosé wine is the colour of the roofs and much of the dusty-red earth. The use of both the plant and the wine can be traced back to the Phoenicians; saffron and rosé are the colours of Provence.

A motorway carves its way through the scrubland. There are glimpses of the sea; there are medieval fortified villages on hill-tops, then there are the vines growing around Bandol. The Domaine Tempier is to be found near the village of Plan de Castellet.

In 1936 Lucie, known as Lulu, Tempier married Lucien Peyraud. It was during the Second World War, with France under occupation by the Germans, that the couple moved their burgeoning young family from Marseilles to the Domaine Tempier, the house and estate of Lulu's father.

'With seven children I had many mouths to feed,' is how Mme Peyraud explains the origin of her love of cooking. She brushes aside the idea that seven children in ten years could be seen as an impediment to fine cooking.

Both the wines and the food here have an international reputation. The American wine-trader Kermit Lynch writes with affection of the legendary Peyraud family hospitality in his book, 'Adventures on the Wine Route'. Mme Peyraud's original and innovative cooking started from a firm base of Provençal traditions and expanded to include recipes and ideas brought back from international travels. It has been a source of inspiration to chefs and writers. The American cookery writer Richard Olney was a neighbour and friend of this domaine and his tribute. 'Lulu's Provençal kitchen' was published in 1995.

The harvest is a time for traditions, not innovation. 'I like to revive all my old repertoire,' explained Mme Peyraud. This estate, which is famous not only for its Rosé but for its fine Bandol Rouge, stopped lodging pickers in 1982 and a few years later Mme Peyraud gave up the cooking for the harvesters. They began to use mainly local families, instead of the students who used to come from other parts of France and farther afield, and for reasons of economy these families prefer to bring and eat a sandwich at lunchtime, and go home to eat in the evening.

They also use, like many other estates, groups of Arabs (nearby Marseilles has a large population of North African Arabs) who bring their own food. So Mme Peyraud would run through her splendid repertoire of such dishes as paella, épaule de mouton aux haricots (shoulder of mutton with beans) and langue de boeuf pot-au-feu (boiled tongue) for un noyau, that is to say some of her family and a permanent team of 6 cavistes (cellar workers) for the fifteen or so days of the harvest, usually the last two weeks of September.

However, the final celebratory meal is for all the pickers as well as friends and family. If the harvest is finished in the evening, it takes place the next day at lunchtime; if the last grapes reach the vat-house in the morning, then the party is in the evening.

Time is needed for one of the two great convivial dishes of Provence to be prepared, and, perhaps, for the exhausted harvesters to build up their strength to participate in la bouillabaise or l'aïoli.

LA BOUILLABAISSE

An exact recipe is a contradiction in terms, it being one of those dishes that depend heavily on what is freshest in the market. Mme Peyraud lists her choice of fish as rascasse (a rock-fish from the Bay of Marseilles), St Pierre (John Dory), vivier (weaver), tranches de fiéla (slices of conger eel), tranches de baudroie (slices of angler fish), des crabes (crabs) and des moules (mussels).

'I put all the fish into a big cauldron with potatoes, tomatoes, garlic, fennel (which grows wild here), saffron and water.' A shortish period of fierce boiling follows, and then: 'everyone has a feast of fish in their own soup bowl,' she ends poetically. Alan Davidson's 'Mediterranean Seafood' is helpful in identifying the fish if you are shopping in the area. The bouillabaisse is accompanied by la sauce rouille (a thick,

Recipes from the French Wine Harvest

reddish-pinkish mayonnaise). Each diner has a deep soup dish full of fish and broth and is served with garlic croûtons (slices of French bread which have been rubbed with garlic, then fried in olive oil or toasted in the oven) and rouille to stir into the broth. To make this mayonnaise, Mme Peyraud first makes an aïoli sauce by pounding garlic to a paste in a stone pestle and mortar, adding egg yolks and, drop by drop, the fruity cold-pressed olive oil. Once the sauce is the consistency of a stiff mayonnaise, she adds pounded saffron, red peppers and monkfish livers.

Aïoli is the name of both a sauce and the dish which it accompanies. Accompanies is perhaps the wrong word. The sauce, for many, is the raison d'être of the dish, and the dish itself not just a meal but an occasion. The French word génial (meaning inspired, having its own genius) seems made for the atmosphere created by this wonderful dish. Properly speaking it is an aïoli garni - a garlic mayonnaise, made with the best local olive oil, with boiled salt cod (previously soaked to get rid of the salt), boiled artichokes, beetroots, carrots, potatoes, cauliflower, green beans all served warm - the selection of cooked vegetables is personal. Mme Peyraud included sweet potatoes, for example, and tomatoes cooked sur la braise (on a wood fire). Very often she added a bowl of poulpe confit (octopus, stewed in red wine with onions and garlic). At the end of the harvest, with everyone relaxing round a table outside, beaucoup de mortiers de sauce (a good many mortars full of sauce) are happily consumed.

If you want to make an aïoli and can get salt cod, allow about 150 g (5 oz) per person. In the markets of Provence two kinds are sold - morue salée et séchée is the traditional salted and dried fish, hard as a board, which can be kept for months and must be soaked in water for 48 hours before cooking, and morue salée, only salted, which needs soaking for 24 hours. In both cases change the water at least 3 or 4 times during the soaking. Poach the fish in fresh water for about 20 minutes and serve, like the vegetables, warm.

If all the vegetables and fish are to come to the table warm, not over-cooked and at the same time, you need plenty of pots and some extra pairs of hands to drain them at the right moment.

Rosi Hanson

The addition of boiled meat and/or a boiled chicken make this into a grand aïoli. Hard-boiled eggs are often included, maybe some soaked and boiled chick peas, and sometimes, cooked snails.

A local person told me she remembered seeing women pickers gathering snails into their aprons as they went through the vines. The snails would then be kept in a cool, dark container and starved to rid them of any impurities, ready to be cooked and added some fifteen to twenty days later, to an aïoli or used to make a cagaoulade, a very local word for a kind of casserole of snails with little bits of bacon, garlic, local white wine, and in some cases, tomatoes.

HARVEST TEA AT THE DOMAINE DU VIEUX TÉLÉGRAPHE

The reputation of the Domaine du Vieux Télégraphe near Bedarrides is a fine one. The wines, mainly red Châteauneuf-du-Pape and also some excellent white, which is unusual, are shipped to many countries, including the U.S.A and the U.K. For their harvest they need 40 to 50 pickers working for three weeks. They use mainly local people, though some come from farther afield, taking some of their holiday entitlement to work in the vines and earn some extra money. Their tradition is to gather everyone together at their farm for a celebratory goûter (literally, tea) at the end.

'In my father-in-law's day,' explained Mme Brunier, wife of the proprietor, 'it really was a tea, with a table spread with cakes, fruit tarts and drinks to be eaten as soon as the workers brought in the last grapes. He always asked me to make des oreillettes.' This is a local expression for bugnes - sweet, delicious, little fritters eaten warm as soon as they are cooked and lifted from the hot oil in which they are deep-fried, and sprinkled with sugar.They are also known locally as cacho-dents (teeth-breakers). They are a very popular regional speciality, also made at Christmas and Easter. As someone else told me, here they take the place of the pancakes and waffles, so beloved by the rest of France. They make a delicious partnership with the local, sweet, white muscat wines of Beaumes de Venise.

Now, though they still call it a goûter, the Bruniers like to celebrate the end of the harvest with a rather more substantial menu.

This area of Provence is famous for its fine lamb. During the day a fire is prepared outside, and two whole milk-fed lambs (agneaux de lait) stuffed with handfuls of thyme which grows wild here, are spit-roasted, and, to give them extra flavour, more herbs are burned on the fire. This must be a mouth-watering sight as the pickers gather for their aperitif.

The first course is usually a selection of salads made from local produce and served in colourful bowls and platters, such as salades niçoises in which bright red tomatoes contrast with the black, small but strong-tasting olives grown nearby; artichoke hearts in oil, roasted red peppers, salads of the local dried pulses (chickpeas, white haricot beans or dark brown Puy lentils) all eaten outside, near to where they are produced, while the smell of lamb and herbs perfumes the air.

With the lamb come the French fries or chips, the current passion for which among pickers in all the regions means they are replacing the more old-fashioned regional potato dishes.

Local cheeses - St Marcellin and the little goat cheeses made here - follow and with them, rather charmingly, 'we give everyone a taste of the wine made from the first grapes picked during the harvest,' says Mme Brunier.

'It is not possible every year - it depends on the weather, and of course the wine is not ready (it may still have some gaz carbonique, making it a little fizzy) but we think the pickers have a special interest in trying the product of their labours. We pick the Syrah grapes at the beginning of the harvest, so that is what we taste.'
If you have an electric rôtisserie or spit roaster, or a charcoal grill or barbecue and would like to cook a leg of lamb, the essential point is to prepare the lamb by inserting slivers of garlic into the meat and rubbing all over with Provençal herbs and olive oil in advance, so that the flavours may penetrate the meat.

Further south the Teisserenc family, who make Vin de Pays des Côtes de Thongue near Béziers, also have a wonderful lamb dish for the end of harvest celebration. In this case a flour and water paste hermetically traditionally seals a leg of lamb in a cast-iron casserole where it cooks very slowly surrounded by fresh figs, walnuts and grapes - all in season locally at the time of the harvest - juniper berries and red wine.

Some years, for a change, the Bruniers serve a Provençal daube (or casserole) of beef. This is also the choice of M. and Mme de Menthon for their celebration at the Château Redortier near Suzette, in the beautiful hills known as Les Dentelles de Montmirail. As Mme de Menthon says - 'A Provençal daube with a good bottle of Gigondas - superb!'

High on a hill facing Mont Ventoux, this family has built a cuverie and a tasting room where they can receive private customers. Here they are offered the wines to taste before buying and are able to admire the spectacular view at the same time.

The thirty hectares of vines producing Côtes-du-Rhône, Beaumes de Venise and Gigondas - all red wines - are planted higher up than most in the region, with their own micro-climate. The de Menthons are often able to look down into the valley which is shrouded in the thick local fog, while their vines are in sunlight, and in several years they have escaped a frost which devastated the lower properties. Their position also means they harvest late, in October and even, on occasion, in November.

M. de Menthon is a native of the Savoie and it is from this Alpine region that he draws his pickers. Each year many of the same friends return; the majority are ski-instructors or mountain guides, who are happy to earn some money picking grapes in their slack season. They usually cook for themselves, provided with ingredients by the proprietors. But on the final night they gather together for that local daube and excellent Gigondas, which they may have helped to pick in previous years.

To precede the daube, Mme de Menthon serves another regional speciality, a tian, prepared by a friend nearby. The tian takes its name from the shallow, round, earthenware dish in which it is cooked and served. The ingredients may be varied, but it is always similar to a kind of vegetable gratin. Courgettes or spinach are often included, sometimes mixed with eggs or thickened with rice or bread. It is often possible to buy ready-cooked tians in the local charcuteries. They are usually topped with breadcrumbs and/or grated cheese, and as they come out of the oven golden and bubbling, they look and smell very appetising. They can also be eaten cold - good outdoor food - and are excellent, hot or cold, accompanied by a fresh tomato sauce. The tian at Château Redortier is one of the most robust, a rich mixture of dried haricot (navy) beans and herbs suitable for the cooler autumn weather.

Some of these tians - the ones which include eggs and green vegetables - are closely related to the cold omelettes which make such a handy snack and were often made by local pickers for their lunch in the vines. Cold omelettes are usually stiff with vegetables and herbs, are not folded in the pan, and, of course, in order to be conveniently portable for a picnic, must not be runny. Local shops sell gâteau de crespeu (sometimes spelt crespeou), a kind of striped orange and green cake or loaf made up of layers of different cold omelettes, the colours coming from the tomatoes, spinach or herbs used in the omelettes. The de Menthon's daube is followed by local goat cheeses and usually a fruit tart, such as apricot, in which locally-picked fruits are arranged on a pastry base, and, after baking, sprinkled with two tablespoons of Muscat Beaumes de Venise, a white dessert wine, to give them extra succulence.

WILD BOAR AND STEEP VINEYARDS IN COTE ROTIE

Bernadette Guigal is a harvest enthusiast. She loves the warm and informal atmosphere amongst the eclectic crowd that make up the picking team at the Maison Guigal in Ampuis, near the ancient town of Vienne. Students, unemployed people, professors, doctors all rub shoulders happily - 'c'est très sympa, tout le monde se tutoie.'

Here, more than anywhere, the pickers need the encouragement of hearty meals because the terraced vineyards are so steep that no machines can get into them and everything must be carried on the back. It is hard to appreciate the spectacular view of the river Rhône when struggling not to lose a footing. A fall sends the basket of grapes cascading down the terraces.

Recipes from the French Wine Harvest

The family business was created in 1946. It was already growing in the 1960s and it was then that Bernadette told her mother-in-law that she thought they ought to be feeding all their 25 harvest workers and that she wanted to take on the job.

The number of pickers more than doubled, as vineyards were acquired over the years, but the cooking was done with just as much zest. 'The food is relatively simple but varied,' says Mme Guigal. She is a great believer in serving dishes full of calories which give the pickers the energy they need (the expression in French is les sucre-lents) - dishes such as gratins of potatoes, or other vegetables, or noodles, all with plenty of cream and cheese. A copious second breakfast is eaten in the vines, and at mid-day there are several services of the main meal back at the house - an entrée of a rice salad or quiche will be followed by a good meat dish, usually roasts with one of those delicious and filling gratins and always a dessert, perhaps a fruit salad with a cake from the local pâtisserie.

The evening meal inevitably starts with soup - 'toujours, toujours, la tradition...,' some cold roast meat, always a hot dish, perhaps an omelette with left-over potatoes, simple meals but nourishing after a hard day. Most popular of all are the game dishes, the product of Marcel Guigal's hobby, served at the weekends during the harvest. With dishes like the splendid civet de sanglier (marinated wild boar) on the menu, no wonder the Guigals' pickers are prepared to risk life and limb on near perpendicular slopes to get the grapes which make the wine that goes into the marinade.

PROVENÇALE GARLIC MAYONNAISE
L'Aïoli

Rosi Hanson

'The magnificent shining gold ointment which is the sauce is often referred to as the beurre de Provence' (Provençal butter) says Elizabeth David in French Provincial Cooking. As this suggests, this sauce is stiff, not pourable.

It is made by pounding garlic in a pestle and mortar (using a machine seems to make it taste bitter) to produce a paste, stirring in egg yolks, then, as for a mayonnaise, adding the best possible (cold-pressed virgin) local olive oil, drop by drop at first, stirring all the while.

As for proportions, Elizabeth David suggests 16 cloves of garlic, 3 egg yolks and 500 ml (nearly a pint) of olive oil for eight people. If you are having a larger party, you might like to know that Mme Peyraud uses three heads of garlic to 10 egg yolks for 30 people.

Lemon juice, salt and pepper are used to season to taste at the end. It is not difficult to make but requires one to be unhurried.

In one version a thick slice of day-old bread is soaked in milk, squeezed and incorporated into the garlic paste before adding the eggs and olive oil. Some people think this stabilises the sauce.
Aïoli is such a good sauce (for garlic lovers) that it is often served with other boiled fish, mixed into soups at the table, mixed into gratins of chickpeas or other vegetables, or served with pot-au-feu.

POTATO AND PARSLEY OMELETTE TO SERVE COLD
Omelette Froide aux Pommes de Terre et Persil

This makes a good lunch when served with a green salad, and is great for picnics.

The recipe is adaptable - use more potatoes if you use fewer eggs, it will still work. Potatoes may be peeled or not as you prefer. Dice them and brown them in olive oil. (Left-over boiled potatoes could be used up as long as they are not mushy). Add plenty of chopped fresh parsley to the lightly-beaten eggs and season with salt and pepper. Tip them into the frying-pan of potatoes and continue as for an ordinary omelette.

At the point when it would normally be served, this omelette must be turned, using a spatula, or if you're brave, flipped like a pancake, and cooked for a few more minutes. If neither of these methods appeal, you could put your pan under a hot grill for a few minutes instead of turning it. Leave to cool.

Rosi Hanson

GRATIN OF HARICOT BEANS

In France red and white haricot beans are sold fresh or semi-dry in the pods, or shelled and dried for the store cupboard. This recipe uses fresh beans but can be adapted for dried ones, by soaking them first overnight and cooking them for longer after the initial soaking in boiling water. It is good, filling, inexpensive food best accompanied by something green and leafy.

FOR 6 - 8 PEOPLE
250 g (8 oz) white haricot beans
250 g (8 oz) red haricot beans
1 onion
2 carrots
bouquet garni of thyme, parsley and bay leaf,
celery stalk, if liked
250 g (8 oz) salt pork or unsmoked
streaky bacon, in a piece
1 tablespoon lard
salt and freshly ground black pepper
a handful of dry breadcrumbs
approximately 30 g (1 oz) butter

Preheat the oven to gas mark 4, 350°F, 180°C.

Shell a mixture of fresh red and white beans. Soak them in boiling water for 15 minutes. Drain and throw away the water. Start again with fresh water. Bring to the boil in a pan. Put in the beans with a peeled onion, the carrots and the bouquet garni. Cover and simmer for aprox. 50 minutes.

Prepare the salt pork or bacon: remove the rind and cut into matchsticks about 0.5 cm (¼ in) wide. Melt a little lard and brown the pork/bacon in it until crisp.

Drain the beans, reserving some of the liquid. Transfer them with the pork, and the poaching vegetables if you wish, to a gratin dish or other shallow ovenproof dish. Season with salt and pepper and moisten with a little of the reserved stock. If you use dried beans you will need a bit more liquid, about 150 ml (¼ pint). Sprinkle a layer of breadcrumbs over the top and dot with butter. Bake in the preheated oven for about an hour. The beans should be meltingly soft, the top crisp.

CHICKPEA SALAD
Salade de Pois Chiches

Chickpeas, like white haricot (navy) beans, are grown in Provence and dried for the store cupboard. The smell of the olive oil as it is mixed with the warm chickpeas is wonderful. This salad is often served as part of a mixed hors d'oeuvre.

Allow 60 g (2 oz) chickpeas per person. Soak the chickpeas in water overnight. Drain and put into a pan covered with fresh water. Bring to the boil. Skim off the scum if you are going to continue to cook them in this water. Otherwise, remove from the heat, leave to cool in the water, drain, rinse under cold water, then cook again in fresh water, salted, and with a bundle of herbs, such as bay, thyme and marjoram, added if liked. Some people think chickpeas indigestible and think that it helps to add a pinch of bicarbonate of soda to the first water in which they are boiled.

The chickpeas may need up two hours slow simmering - test to see if they are soft - it is hard to be exact. Drain. While warm, dress with olive oil, plenty of salt and freshly ground black pepper, a handful of parsley finely chopped and lemon juice to taste. Chopped mild onion is often added.

MACARONI CHEESE THE FRENCH WAY
Gratin de Nouilles

This is the sort of dish so popular during the grape-harvest - filling and energy giving. Similar gratins are made with vegetables such as chard stalks or celery. It is a simple formula which can be adapted.

FOR 4 - 6 PEOPLE
(depending on whether served alone or with a meat dish)
250 g (8 oz) macaroni
100g (3½ oz) grated Gruyère
45 g (1½ oz) butter
200 ml (7 fl oz) crème fraîche
salt, pepper, freshly grated nutmeg

Preheat the oven to gas mark 7, 425°F, 220°C.

Cook the macaroni in a large pot of boiling salted water. Drain thoroughly.

Butter a gratin dish. Put in half the macaroni, half the cheese scattered over them and half the crème fraîche. Season with pepper and grate some nutmeg over them. Cover with the remaining macaroni, cheese and crème fraîche.

Bake in the hot oven for about 30 minutes, till bubbling and brown on top.

Recipes from the French Wine Harvest

MARIE-PIERRE TEISSERENC'S LEG OF LAMB SLOW COOKED IN RED WINE WITH FIGS, WALNUTS AND GRAPES

Gigot d'Agneau aux Figues, Noix et Raisins Blancs

A wonderful combination of flavours, this is a great dish for early September when fresh walnuts and figs are in season.

FOR 8 - 10 PEOPLE
1 onion
1 carrot
olive oil
1 leg of lamb, about 2 kg (4 lb)
Salt
fresh figs (white or black), about 1 per person
white grapes, about 500 g (1 lb)
fresh walnuts, about 500g (1 lb)
a few juniper berries
2 glasses of red wine
flour and water for a paste to seal the casserole (or use tinfoil/aluminium)

Preheat the oven to gas mark 4, 350°F, 180°C.

Peel and chop the onion and carrot. Heat a little oil in the casserole - choose one which is just big enough for the lamb and for the other ingredients to fit round it. Season the lamb with salt and brown in the oil with the onion and carrot. Turn from time to time so all sides are sealed in the heat - it will take about 20 minutes. Wash the figs and grapes. Roughly chop the figs. De-pip the grapes, if you so wish. Crack the nut shells and remove the walnuts, peeling off as much of the bitter skins as possible. Chop them roughly. Add all to the casserole round the lamb. Add the juniper berries and the red wine.

When the wine comes to the simmer, put a layer of tin-foil/aluminium and the lid so it is well sealed.

Traditionally a flour and water paste was used to seal the lid. Should you wish to do this, here are the instructions: In a bowl put 500 g (1 lb) plain flour and stir in about 300 ml (10 fl oz) water. As an example, this amount will be enough to seal the lid of a Le Creuset oval casserole size H. Mix to a stiff paste (best done with the hands, a messy but quite pleasant business - a good moment to involve a child). Put the lid on the casserole. Off the heat press the paste all round the edge.

Put the lamb into the preheated oven and leave for 2 ½ hours.

When the time comes to serve the lamb, if you have made a paste, now is the time to chip it off being careful to remove it all before opening the lid in case some falls in.

Let the lamb rest for 10-15 minutes in a warm place before carving it and arranging it with the fruit and nuts and its sauce of red wine and cooking juices in a deep serving dish.

MME PEYRAUD'S PAËLLA WITH FISH, CHICKEN AND RABBIT

'There is no typical version,' said Mme Peyraud. Smiling, she added, 'you can do anything you like in cooking.' How reassuring! Some people seek to mystify; here is one of France's great cooks setting us free to use our heads and sense of taste.

Recipes from the French Wine Harvest

I have suggested using cooked prawns and langoustines because this is what is most widely available. Simple to make, this is an adaptable party dish, usually made in large quantities, so amounts are flexible.

Fish - your choice, but Mme Peyraud uses monkfish because it is firm-fleshed; other firm white fish would be suitable; cut into bite-sized cubes, and allow 2 to 3 per person

Sea-food - large cooked prawns and/or langoustines in their shells, one of each per person. Mussels could also be used, allowing 4 to 6 per person. (Should be alive when bought - scrub and scrape the shells to get rid of sand, grit and mud, pull off the 'beards'. Discard any with broken or open shells.

Bring a little water to boil in a large pan, put in the mussels and with the lid on steam them until they open, about 5 to 8 minutes.)

meat - 1 chicken leg or thigh per person or 1 - 2 pieces of rabbit per person
rice - 1 rounded tablespoon per person: in Provence they use a long
    grain rice grown locally in the Carmargue area
onions - 1 medium per 6 people
garlic - 2 to 3 cloves per 6 people
tomatoes if liked (not worth including if not really ripe and full of
    flavour), 250 - 500 g (½ - 1 lb) per 6 people
a good pinch of powdered saffron
a good pinch of ground aniseed
salt and black pepper
olive oil
boiling water - about twice as much as the volume of rice

Take a large frying-pan or shallow sauté pan (unless you have a paella pan) and in it heat enough olive oil to coat the bottom lightly. Brown the pieces of fish, and put aside. Now brown the chicken or rabbit and continue cooking in the oil for about 15-20 mins. Add the peeled, chopped onion and garlic. Peel and chop the tomatoes, if using them, and sauté for a few minutes in the pan.

Cover all these ingredients with boiling water and cook gently for about 20 mins. Add the saffron (and make sure when you buy it that it is a good saffron and not a substitute), aniseed, salt and pepper. Add 1 tablespoon of rice per person. Stir, turn down the heat and simmer gently for about 20 minutes. The rice should absorb the water in that time.

Test and if you feel the rice is still not quite cooked add a little more hot water and continue cooking for a few minutes.

Towards the end of the cooking add the fish to finish cooking for about 5 mins, and the cooked prawns, langoustines and mussels or clams in their shells, to heat through.

The colours and flavours of this dish are most enticing.

Rosi Hanson

SLOW COOKED PROVENÇALE BEEF
Daube Provençale

This recipe is based on the one used by Mme Brunier from 'La Cuisine Provençale' by J. B. Rebouil, thought of locally as the cooking Bible.

What makes a daube, a daube? This dish, which crops up on almost all harvest menus, is perfect for feeding a large party. Preparations must be made in advance, and all authorities seem to agree that the flavours improve and develop on reheating, which makes it convenient. Is there a definitive version? Surely not. Everyone who makes it has a favourite recipe, from which over years they may have deviated without noticing. The use of local wine, orange zest for seasoning (only a small thing but the taste comes through subtly) and spices such as cloves, juniper berries and allspice, make this version Provençale, but there are many other versions.

Many recipes start by frying diced streaky bacon, and in some the meat is larded with little bits of bacon fat. Tastes have moved away from dishes with a lot of fat; meat is being produced with as little fat as possible now, but it is important for the meat in these dishes requiring long, slow cooking to have some fat, otherwise it will become dry and stringy, instead of soft and melting.

There are two points worth noting. The first concerns the wine for the marinade, and ultimately for the cooking: the better the quality, the better the end result. The ladies of whom I am writing have the advantage that good wine is always available to them. But for us who have to buy our cooking wine, it is better to save money by buying cheaper cuts of meat than poor quality wine. The truth is that industrialised, mass-produced bottles of neutral wine result in thin, unpleasant sauces. Naturally this does not mean that you must buy a First Growth for your daube, just that it is better not to cook with anything you would not be happy to drink.

The second point concerns the browning of the meat (and this applies whether a recipe calls for meat in one piece or diced). All the French women I have watched making this kind of dish have insisted that this step is vitally important to the success of the dish, and not just because browned meat looks more appetising. They get whatever fat or oil they are using smoking hot; they themselves get very hot, and probably spattered with fat doing it, but consider it worth it.

The technical reasons are well described in some detail in Part 1 of the translated edition of Escoffier's 'Guide Culinaire', for those who would like to understand the process better. But, in essence, this searing of the meat allows the long cooking to soften the fibres gradually without ruining the texture of the meat. The only other thing to say is that making a daube is not difficult, but it does need care and attention to detail - the result is a dish of wonderful flavours.

FOR 8 PEOPLE
2 kg (4 lb) stewing beef - cuts with
some fat, such as top rump, or silverside or even
brisket (U.K.) or a boneless pot roast, such as chuck
underblade (U.S.A.) are suitable
200g (7 oz) pork fat or 125 g (4 oz) lard
1 onion, roughly chopped
4 - 5 cloves garlic
a piece of orange zest

FOR THE MARINADE:
2 onions, cut in quarters,
2 - 3 carrots, peeled and roughly chopped
a bouquet garni (bay leaf, thyme and parsley tied in a
little bunch, with a stick of celery if liked)
salt, peppercorns and other spices (4 - 5 juniper berries,
2 - 3 cloves, 4 - 5 allspice berries)
1 bottle red wine (here Côtes-du-Rhône would probably be used)
1 small glass red wine vinegar

NB start at least 24 hours ahead – allowing time for marinading, slow cooking, and if wished, reheating.

Cut up the meat into large cubes weighing about 125 g (aprox 4 oz) each. Put them with the marinade ingredients into a bowl and leave for 6 hours in a cool place, or overnight in the refrigerator.
Drain the meat and vegetables, reserving the liquid. Place the liquid in a pan and boil hard to reduce by half. Skim off any scum as it boils.

Dry the pieces of meat carefully. This is important as they will not brown successfully if wet.
Melt the fat in a pan. If using pork fat, lift out any resulting little balls of frizzled fat which have not melted, using a skimmer. Brown the onion gently in the fat and set aside.

Let the fat get very hot and brown the pieces of meat well on both sides in batches. You may find it easier to do this in a heavy-based frying-pan, transferring the meat to a casserole once browned. Add a little of the marinade to the caramelised juices in the pan, stir and pour into the casserole. (An enamelled cast-iron casserole is ideal.)

Add 4 or 5 cloves of garlic, the orange zest, and the vegetables, herbs and spices from the marinade. Pour over the reduced marinade, adding a cup of warm water. The meat should not be completely drowned. Cover with foil and the casserole lid and simmer very gently. Timing depends on the cut of meat used; it is best to check after 3 ½ hours. (The most economical cuts need a bit longer) Baste the top of the meat with the liquid from time to time, so that it does not dry out if it is not quite covered. Remove any fat before serving - this is much easier to do if the daube is allowed to cool so that the fat rises to the top and can be spooned off; it can be reheated when needed. You may also like to remove the orange peel and bouquet garni.

Mme Brunier says the daube should be served very hot and goes well with boiled potatoes or fresh pasta. She adds black olives towards the end of the cooking.

Many cooks thicken the sauce. After browning the meat, sprinkle with a little flour and cook briefly before adding the marinade. Or add a beurre manié (a spoon full of flour mixed into the same of butter) just before the end of the cooking. If you prefer a sauce with more body but do not wish to add flour, you could drain it from the meat and reduce it a little by boiling in an open pan, before reuniting with the dish and serving.

LEG OF PORK OR WILD BOAR MARINADED IN RED WINE
Civet de Sanglier

Mme Guigal marinades legs of local wild boar in some of the domaine's excellent Côte Rôtie with salt, pepper, cloves, thyme, bay leaves, onion, garlic, carrots, a little olive oil and cognac for 48 hours. While the meat is roasting she reduces the marinade to make a sauce. As she points out, the longer wine cooks, the more its natural acidity predominates. This is corrected by adding some redcurrant jelly and a little cream at the end.

The following recipe is an adaptation to use with leg of pork. It works well, and the sauce, a glowing dark red, is deliciously winey.

FOR 10 - 12 PEOPLE
half a leg of pork, weighing about 3 kg (6 lb),
rind removed

FOR THE MARINADE:
1 onion, stuck with 3 or 4 cloves
2 - 3 carrots, roughly chopped
2 bottles red wine (the Guigals can use Côte Rôtie, or
Côte du Rhône but this is expensive. Alternatively, a

wine from the Midi such as a Vin de Pays d'Oc, or a Shiraz from Australia would give a good result)
2 - 3 cloves of garlic
2 bay leaves
bunch of fresh or dried thyme sprigs
2 tablespoons olive oil
2 - 3 tablespoons cognac
salt
6 black peppercorns

FOR THE SAUCE:
1 teaspoon of cornflour
approximately 1 tablespoon redcurrant jelly
4-5 tablespoons pouring cream
salt and black pepper

Place the marinade ingredients and the pork in a large bowl. Leave it somewhere cool for 48 hours. If you have to put it in the fridge, allow a day longer.

When you come to cook it, have the oven preheated to gas mark 4, 350°F, 180°C.

Lift the pork from the marinade, drain and put it straight, into a baking tin and into the oven. Roast for 30 to 35 minutes per half kilo (1 lb), in this case about 3 hours.

To make the sauce, sieve the marinade into a pan - avoid aluminium which will react with the wine. Boil the liquid, uncovered, to reduce it by about half, skimming off the rather unappetising looking scum that comes to the top. Allow about 20 to 30 minutes for this.

Put a teaspoon of cornflour in a little bowl, add a small ladle of the reduced marinade and mix until smooth. Add this to the pan and let it simmer, stirring for about five minutes.

Taste, Stir in half the redcurrant jelly, then taste again. Add the rest of the redcurrant if needed. Add the cream. Taste once more and add salt and pepper as you think fit.

While you are working on the sauce, take the pork out of the oven and let it rest. Carve and arrange on a dish. Pour the sauce over it and serve.

SHOULDER OF LAMB COOKED IN RED WINE WITH GARLIC & HERBS, WITH DRIED HARICOT BEANS
Epaule d'Agneau aux Haricots

The shoulder is braised in a large, heavy, covered casserole, with carrots, onions, wine, stock, garlic and herbs. Dried haricot beans are partly cooked, then added to the casserole towards the end of the cooking, taking on the mingled flavours of the other ingredients and becoming soft and melting. Usually served as it is without any other vegetables.

FOR 8 PEOPLE
1 shoulder of lamb, weighing about 2½ kg (5 lb)
a little olive oil
2 large carrots
2 medium onions
approximately 250 ml (8 fl oz) local red wine
(Côtes de Rhône for example)
salt and pepper
2 large cloves of garlic
1 bay leaf
1 teaspoon of dried thyme, or a small bunch
of fresh thyme,
1 tablespoon of tomato paste
600 ml (1 pint) stock (chicken is suitable)
500g (1 lb) dried haricot beans

The day before: wash the beans, pick out any stones, and soak overnight.

Preheat the oven to gas mark 4, 350°F, 180°C.

Trim off any extra fat on the meat. Heat the olive oil in the casserole (which should be just big enough for the meat and vegetables round it). When it is hot, brown the meat, turning from time to time for about 20 minutes.

Meanwhile, prepare the carrots and onions by peeling and slicing them.

Remove the lamb while you brown the vegetables in the oil for a few minutes, stirring them so that they do not burn. Put them on one side. If there is a lot of oil, or the lamb has produced a lot of fat, pour it off. Deglaze the pan with the wine, stirring at first to dislodge any bits from the meat or vegetables, then let it boil to reduce by about half.

Season the lamb with salt and freshly ground black pepper.

Add the lamb and vegetables to the wine. Peel the garlic and gently crush under the wide blade of a knife. Add the garlic, bay leaf, thyme and tomato paste to the casserole. Add stock till it comes about half-way up the lamb. Let it simmer gently for a few minutes, cover with foil and the lid and move to the oven. Cooking time is about 2½ hours, but after about half an hour check to see if it is cooking too fast - it should only simmer gently - and turn down the heat if necessary. Take the opportunity to spoon some of the liquid over the meat. Do the same when you add the partly-cooked beans, after a further 1½ hours.

To cook the beans, drain them, put into a saucepan and cover with cold water (no salt). Bring to the boil. White scum will be produced and can be skimmed off. Reduce the heat, cover and simmer for 45 to 60 minutes. It is difficult to be accurate about the timing; if they are old they may need a bit longer. They should be just slightly undercooked at this stage. Leave them in their cooking water until you are ready to drain and add them to the casserole for the final half hour of cooking round the lamb in the oven.

To serve, after resting carve the lamb, arrange it with the beans and braising vegetables on a dish and pour over some of the cooking liquid.

SWEET CRISP FRITTERS
Oreillettes

500 g (1 lb) plain flour
4 egg yolks
150 g (5 oz) caster sugar
2 teaspoons orange-flower water
100 ml (3½ oz) water
approximately 60 - 125g (2 - 4 oz) unsalted butter, if using, melted and cooled
oil for deep-frying

Sieve the flour onto a pastry-board. Make a well in the centre and put in the egg yolks, sugar, orange-flower water and water. At this point you can add some melted butter. Mix into a dough and leave to rest for an hour or two.

Divide into pieces weighing approximately 60 g (2 oz) each. Working with one piece at a time, roll out on a floured surface, to a thickness of barely 2 mm (1½ in). Using a pastry-wheel, cut diagonally to make thin ribbons. Traditionally these are formed into a ring shape but this is not necessary.

The final stage requires a deep-fryer of hot oil. Tip in the ribbons in batches. As soon as they turn golden-brown, lift out with a slotted spoon and sprinkle with sugar.

Eat immediately.

APRICOT TART SPRINKLED WITH MUSCAT BEAUMES DE VENISE
Tarte aux abricots arrosée de Muscat Beaumes de Venise

This lovely tart is served at Château Redortier - both the fruit and the sweet aromatic wine are local - at the end of harvest celebration meal.

FOR 6 - 8 PEOPLE
FOR THE SWEET SHORTCRUST PASTRY
(to fill a 25 cm (10 in) tart tin):
200g (7 oz) plain flour
1 small pinch of salt
about 15 g (1 oz) caster sugar
100 g (3½ oz) butter at room temperature
1 egg
a little water

FOR THE FILLING:
750 g - 1 kg (1½ - 2 lb) ripe apricots
 1 tablespoon sugar,
optional 2 - 3 tablespoons Muscat Beaumes de Venise,
(keep the rest of the bottle to drink with the tart)
1 egg yolk, optional

Preheat the oven to gas mark 6, 400°F, 200°C, with a heavy baking sheet on the middle shelf.

Sift the flour into a large bowl with the salt and sugar. Roughly cut up the butter, then with the tips of your fingers, speedily rub it into the flour until it looks like breadcrumbs.

Lightly beat the egg with about a teaspoon of cold water. Make a dip in the middle of the heap of flour, pour in the egg and mix until it is a supple and moist paste. Form this into a ball, cover and leave to rest for an hour.

Butter a 25 cm (10 in) removable-base, fluted tart tin. Roll out the pastry on a floured surface and line the tart tin with it. Chill for 1 hour.

Cover the pastry with a piece of buttered baking parchment, weighted with dried beans. Put into the preheated oven on the baking sheet for about 8 minutes. Remove the paper and beans. Prick the base of the pastry with a fork and return to the oven for about 3 minutes more. It should be just starting to come away from the sides of the tin; do not let it get too brown.

Reduce the oven heat to gas mark 4, 350°F, 180°C.

Stone the fruit and slice thinly. If they are under-ripe, it might be worth poaching the slices for a few minutes in a little water and sugar but you must drain them carefully.

Arrange them in concentric circles in the pastry shell. In order to prevent the pastry becoming soggy, many people like to brush the base with egg yolk before doing this. Sprinkle the fruit with the tablespoon of sugar if using.

Bake in the preheated oven for about 20 minutes. This tart is nice served warm, but whether eaten warm or cold, sprinkle the fruit with the Muscat Beaumes de Venise just before serving. It should make a sensational finish to the meal.

BORDEAUX

Bordeaux used to be the very bastion of British snobbism about "claret" as the red wine was traditionally known in the UK. Eleanor of Aquitaine had brought this region to the English crown by her marriage to Henry II in 1152. The fact that the Earl of Shrewsbury was defeated by the French in 1453 - thereby losing the territory – did not, happily, weaken the trading connection in the long term, and now sales of Bordeaux at all levels are as strong as ever in Britain.

Bordeaux is a great city, officially the second most beautiful in France after Paris; it is the most sophisticated wine capital in France. The old town near the river dates principally from the seventeenth and eighteenth centuries. The magnificent architecture of the quays alongside the Gironde reflects the commercial confidence of that era. It is still a busy port. In the city centre it is a pleasure to stroll down the elegant Allées de Tourny and to sit in a glassed-in pavement brasserie, eating local oysters and omelette aux cèpes (wild mushroom omelette). The opera house is across the street; posters advertise plays, concerts or a new exhibition at one of the museums. A short walk away some of the best food produce in the world can be bought (not cheaply, of course) in and around the modern, covered market, Le Marché des Grands Hommes. Vegetables and fruit from nearby Spain, an astonishing array of fish and seafood from the Atlantic, the best meat, all the most luxurious products of Périgord, such as foie gras and confit d'oie; specialist cheese shops. Among the cheeses from all over France it is a surprise to find the big round balls of aged Dutch Gouda which are a speciality here. Then there are shops where they have perfected the art of hand-making chocolates. The citizens of Bordeaux can eat, as well as drink, like kings.

Access to the Atlantic meant that the Bordelais were exporting wines many years before land-locked regions, such as Burgundy. But the Bordeaux merchants have had their downs as well as their ups. Towards the end of the nineteenth century the phylloxera, a louse which attacks the roots and ultimately kills the vines, was responsible for enormous damage (in other areas too), with all the financial implications from the subsequent uprooting of the vineyards and the re-planting with resistant stock from America, where the louse originated. Vines take at least four years to produce a crop and many years to reach maturity. Although most farmers are natural grumblers, this really was a devastating set-back.

In 1956 frost killed many of the vines. Again there had to be re-planting.

Then, in 1973, the Bordeaux market collapsed spectacularly. There had been two boom years when there hardly seemed enough wine to satisfy the market, despite the huge production of the area. Prices soared for the great vintages, then high prices began to be asked, and paid, for the poor vintages. Speculators came into the market - wines were being bought and sold for huge prices, not for drinking but as an international commodity. You might think it would be easy to see this must end in tears, but the atmosphere at that time was a frenetic and heady one. Then came the oil crisis and economic recession. The bottom dropped out of the market. Merchants were left holding large stocks of wine no-one seemed to want. Some went under, and most took years to recover from the financial disaster. Now that the wines from Bordeaux's greatest châteaux are sold for astronomic prices to collectors all over the globe, that may seem a distant memory.

Bordeaux is the most important area on the globe for the production of the full range of table wine styles. There are dry white wines ranging from cheap to expensive and the famous sweet dessert white wines of Sauternes and Barsac. Among the reds there is everyday-drinking plonk which sells at reasonable prices, a broad spectrum of mid-price, high quality wine, and, of course, the very finest bottles from world famous châteaux.

All through the eighties, the spread of wine-making skills in the area resulted in much greater production of high quality wines. More people were studying oenology, the science of wine-making, at the University of Bordeaux in Talence, as indeed they were at the University of Dijon in Burgundy. Professors Peynaud and Ribereau-Gayon, indefatigable in their pursuit of quality, were signed up as wine-making consultants to dozens of leading properties. Fine wine from Bordeaux is no longer rare, but even so, the well-known châteaux have stayed consistently expensive. Other parts of the world have planted the classic Bordeaux vine types and universities in America and Australia also produce good oenologists; a new, well-informed wine-drinking public is willing to experiment. Perhaps Bordeaux is no longer in a position to be complacent.

The wine area known as Bordeaux is extremely large and is made up of a number of distinct vineyard areas, each with its own character derived from the different soils and micro-climates. When you realise that it is at least 120 miles from the tip of the Médoc, situated on the peninsular north of the city, to the Sauternes and Barsac vineyards in the south, you understand the scale of the place. It is also understandable that several different grape types are planted to suit the different conditions. Most wines are made from a blend of different vines planted in the same vineyard.

The Sauvignon Blanc is a grape which brings fruitiness to the dry whites. The other classic white Bordeaux grape is the Semillon, which produces a rich, broad-flavoured wine that ages well. When climatic conditions are right, Semillon is attacked by 'noble rot', which has the benign effect of concentrating the sugar in the fruit and results in the production of luscious dessert wines.

There are three main red grape types. The first is the Cabernet Sauvignon. It gives deep purple-red wine with its own intense character and relatively strong tannins. It is the backbone of the character of the wines of the Médoc and gives them their legendary ageing ability. Equally important is the Merlot which produces a more supple, very ripe wine and is widely planted in all the regional appellations, such as Côtes de Castillon, Côtes de Bourg and Premières Côtes de Bordeaux. Merlot is also the grape which gives fleshiness and flavour to the best wines of Pomerol and Fronsac. Thirdly, there is the Cabernet Franc, which is particularly planted around St Emilion. It is this grape which, when vinified with the Merlot, can produce superbly balanced wines suitable to be enjoyed while young, as well as ageing elegantly.

There is a bewildering number of châteaux (and the word 'château' covers a variety of different buildings, by no means all of them on a grand scale, and some of them uninhabited). In 1855 the first major classification of some of the best châteaux was made. In the Médoc, the villages of Margaux. St Julien, Pauillac and St Estephe were covered, and for the dessert wines, Sauternes and Barsac. At the top there were four: Lafite, Latour, Margaux and one outsider: Haut Brion in the Graves area was judged to be so exceptional that it had to be included in this select band of First Growths. Château d'Yquem headed the classification in Sauternes. Much later, in 1973, Mouton Rothschild was elevated to the First Growths.

St Emilion had to wait a hundred years to be classified, Cheval Blanc and Ausone being recognised as First Great Growths. Recently it has been re-classified and even now there are disputes. Some outstanding areas have never been classified, for instance, Canon Fronsac and Pomerol, but in the latter it has long been acknowledged that Pétrus is on the same level as the Médoc First Growths.

Many of the lesser known areas, where they are now making the best value wines of all, are completely uncharted waters. It is difficult to make sense of all this - with the result that it has kept many experts in business for years!

Rosi Hanson

HARVEST RITES

It is autumn and it is misty, easy to miss a turning in this unsigned country, where little roads meander between large vineyards. Leaving behind the suburbs of the market town of Libourne on the banks of the wide Dordogne river, villages are not much more than a cluster of buildings around a crossroads. Sometimes one glimpses a small château behind a stand of trees. The impression is that vines are more important than houses here.

Driving at dusk down a straight country road in Pomerol a strange sight meets the eyes. A bonfire is blazing. As the flames die down, a team of sturdy women approach it, carrying a large contraption on long poles. Like high-priestesses in a pagan ritual, they lower it onto the embers, then stand back. In the falling light, figures are emerging from the anonymous farm buildings, to stand around the fire. The ladies advance again, in formation. They lift the contraption off the fire, and, wielding forks, fall on the sausages grilling on it to turn them. A delicious smell from the burning dried vine shoots and grilling meat wafts across the courtyard encouraging the pickers to hurry in to dinner.

There is a 120-strong team here. The family business Jean-Pierre Moueix, which owns 48.3 ha in Pomerol and 23.5 ha in St. Emilion, including La Fleur-Petrus, Trotanoy, Hosanna, and Belair Monange, makes sure that they are well-fed, in a refectory designed by the Swiss architects Herzog & de Meuron, of Tate Modern fame. Christian Moueix produces a special cuvee of red wine for the harvesters, available at breakfast, lunch and dinner in generous quantities. His wife, Cherise, enthuses about the many activities they organise for the pickers. Spanish night with singers, paella and sangria, an evening of choucroute and draft beer, belote and petanque competitions, loto, and bandas night with a brass and percussion band, all ensure that pickers want to return annually.

In the vines of La Fleur Gazin, the swallows appear to be dive-bombing the pickers as they swoop low over the vines, eating little insects stirred up as the leaves are parted. When the last grapes of the harvest are loaded, the tractor sets off for the chai (vat-house), decorated with flowers. There are squeals and shouts as one or two pickers are set upon, dragged to the truck and thrown into the sticky mass - you get the feeling some scores are being settled. A large jar of wine is passed round and the Chef de Culture sets off a rocket to signal the end of the work. It is time for lunch and a hard-earned break before the celebration dinner.

The atmosphere is convivial - cars and trucks moved to make way for a fireworks display, a local band is setting up in the refectory and the cooks' helpers are arranging posies of flowers in jam-jars, jugs, or anything else to hand, to make the tables festive. Confetti, hats and horns will be distributed to add to the fun. From the gerbe or sheaf of flowers, traditionally offered by the workers to the owners at the end of the harvest, comes the Bordelais name for the celebration, gerbebaude.

Christian Moueix, sitting at the head of one of the tables, is surrounded by his team of Oenologist, Chef de Culture, Maître de Chai, Régisseur and Export Director, all of whom will respond to chanted requests for a song as the night wears on and the wine flows. But now, before the inevitable soup - which today will be followed by bouchées à la reine (flaky pastry vol-au-vents filled with seafood in a creamy sauce) before duck breasts grilled over vine shoots - the band strikes up a fanfare, and in comes a delegation of the pickers with bouquets of flowers for the owner and the cooks.

Do things taste better grilled over Cabernet or Merlot vine shoots? This esoteric question has little relevance in most of our lives, but here in the Bordeaux region it can generate a lively debate as there are vine shoots (sarments) in abundance, kept from the time of pruning. The flavour they impart to meat or fish is delicious and during the harvest some of the best meals are of sausages, brochettes (cubes of veal or lamb interspersed with bacon on skewers), fresh sardines, pork chops, or thin slices of pork breast known as du lard or ventreche, all grilled sur sarments. It is typically local.

Many châteaux continue to use traditional cooking methods. At Château Figeac, for instance, they use huge old cauldrons over wood fires for their soups and for pot-au-feu. This lovely property, which is a Premier Grand Cru Classé in the St Emilion area, is renowned not only for its wine but also for its spectacular gerbebaude. There are games and sports and one famous year there were circus people amongst the harvesters, who did trapeze acts in the courtyard. A band of gypsies, who return each year to pick the grapes, perform traditional dances.

GOOD FOOD AND THE BEST NIGHT-CLUB IN TOWN

A tantalising smell of grilling meat leads to a charming room across a little garden. Mme Chabrerie has worked at Château Haut Sarpe for many years and her husband is Chef de Culture. This morning she is grilling steaks - huge pieces of meat from cattle raised on the farm (two cows are killed for the harvest) over vine shoots in a renaissance fireplace. On cold evenings the harvesters come in here to warm up with vin chaud (hot wine, with sugar and spices) and roast chestnuts on the fire. Mme Chabrerie sprinkles chopped shallots over each batch of steak (entrecôte à la bordelaise), as she takes them off the fire. It is hot work and she must be glad of a breath of fresh air as she walks back across the garden to the harvest kitchen, next to the beautiful refectory with its old beams and little decorative touches so typical of this family estate.

The emphasis here is on family values and respect for tradition. The attention to detail is astonishing, both in the running of the estate and the way the harvesters are looked after. The Janoueix family is actively involved in running the estate; they own several other fine properties and a merchant business in Libourne. Before the harvest every picker, about 130 in all, receives a charming letter welcoming them and telling them what is expected of them and what they can expect in return. Many of the pickers are sons and daughters of customers.

Everyone receives a certificate and two bottles of the estate's wine to take home; there are prizes awarded for the best male and female pickers and special awards to long-serving harvesters, presented during a terrific party on the last night.

Lunch is on the tables and the pickers are coming in. Mme Janoueix, carrying a plastic bag full of medicines and other remedies, is searching out the ones who need nursing over a cold or a gastric problem. Vegetable soup is warming after a rather cold morning in the vines. Some people practise the old peasant habit (known as faire Chabrot) of adding a large glass of wine to the last of their soup. A salad of beetroot and some pâté follows, and then the splendid entrecôtes à la bordelaise and big plates of frîtes. All the vegetables and salads are grown on the estate; the poultry and meat used during the harvest are raised here and the pâtés are home-made from the pigs on the farm. The Janoueix's try to serve as many local dishes as possible for their pickers. There is even one dish, oeufs et braganes en sauce au vin, made from eggs and little wild leeks that grow between the rows of vines. As the meal is coming to an end, with cheese and crème renversée, an impromptu concert starts up - the instruments are only bottles and cutlery, but it is coming from a team of young Danes who have obviously been practising and it sounds good.

Haut Sarpe is unusual in being able to lodge all its pickers in a lovely collection of old farm buildings, a sort of harvest village, with the kitchen and refectory at its centre. There is a benignly paternal atmosphere generated by the family. Leather-bound albums of photographs record past harvests and are regularly added to; a photo-collage of the last year's harvest is on show in the refectory. The family are always pleased when marriages result from harvest encounters, as they often do. Indeed Jean Janoueix met his own wife when she came to pick the harvest as a young woman; now their own children are part of the team.

With a high proportion of young people picking the harvest here, the Janoueix's try hard to make every night a party night. Often there are fancy-dress competitions and this picturesque harvest hamlet's very own disco, the 'Glu-glu-glu', opens after dinner until midnight. 'It's the best night-club in town!' they say and it is probably the only one in the world situated in the middle of vineyards. The music wafts across the courtyard, waking the ducks on the pond and the peacocks in the park of the château; the old buildings look even prettier in the moonlight. It is easy to see how marriages are made at Haut Sarpe.

Rosi Hanson

ENTRECOTE A LA BORDELAISE

A hungry cellar-worker grilling a steak over an improvised fire made from the staves of old barrels steeped in the tannins of Bordeaux wines: these are the supposed origins of this celebrated dish. Who or when are facts that are lost in the usual mists of time. But there are stories of esteemed gastronomes of the past being glad to accept an invitation from a cellar master to share an entrecôte cooked in this way. However, barrels are expensive things nowadays and châteaux are more likely to be selling their old ones than letting their workers use them as cooking fuel. In any case, it gradually became the tradition to use vine-shoots (sarments) saved from the pruning, or old vine stocks taken out during re-planting, to make the fire. The ingredients are few and simple but the combination of steak, shallots and bone marrow has become a classic.

According to an often-quoted old book ('Traîté de Cuisine Bourgeoise Bordelaise' by Alcide Bontou), the piece of steak should be about the thickness of two fingers. It should be marinaded in a tablespoon of oil, salt and freshly-ground black pepper. When the fire is glowing, put the meat on the grill. Chop together 4 shallots, a good firm piece of beef marrow and a little handful of parsley. Turn the steak and spread this mixture over the upper surface. Heat the blade of the knife and use it to press down the mixture a few times, to soften the marrow. That is all. Any other complications, such as red wine sauces, which sometimes go under the name of entrecôtes à la bordelaise, are usually denounced as not being the real thing. (Though they may be a perfectly good thing in their own right - the entrecôte is usually fried in a pan and kept warm while chopped shallots are briefly tossed in the same butter. A teaspoon of flour is then added and a sauce made by adding a glass each of red wine and water, to which chopped, raw marrow is added and softened in it. This sometimes appears as entrecôte marchand du vin.)

It is useful to know how to prepare the marrow. The marrow bone should be sawn into 7.5 cm (3 in) lengths by the butcher. If possible, soak the pieces in cold water for 12 to 24 hours, changing the water several times. Put the bones in cold water to cover, bring slowly to the boil and allow to barely simmer for about 20 minutes. Scoop the marrow out of the bone with the handle of a small spoon. Marrow bones vary in size. Ask the butcher for advice on quantities. It is now ready to chop with the shallots and parsley.

If no marrow bones are obtainable, all is not lost. In the Bordeaux area you see people grilling steaks and simply sprinkling them with a good handful of chopped shallots and parsley.

IN THE LAND OF THE REALLY GRAND CHATEAUX

The Médoc takes its name from the Latin in medio aquae - it lies between the Atlantic Ocean and the Gironde Estuary. It is flat and the soil is poor - it is a curious fact that vines thrive on the poorest soil, and you see little other vegetation apart from the characteristic pines along the Atlantic coast. If you are in the Médoc you are bound to be on either business or pleasure connected with wine; nothing else seems to happen here and it is on the way to nowhere, unless you count crossing the estuary by ferry.

For many people Margaux, St Julien and the other villages of the Haut-Médoc, with their imposing châteaux and extensive vineyards, epitomise great Bordeaux wines. A large number are owned by absentee landlords - American, Japanese and English multi-national corporations put in managers to run these valuable investments. Now the Chinese are beginning to snap up lesser known properties. There is no doubt that this creates a different atmosphere from that of the smaller, family-owned properties around Libourne.

As you drive through the immaculately tended vines, with a rose-bush at the end of each row, there is a plethora of signs with famous names. It seems as if some kind of architectural competition has taken place here, so varied are the styles. They range from the beautiful eighteenth century Château Beychevelle, to the ultra grand Château Ducru Beaucaillou, to the Chinese pagoda-like folly which is Cos d'Estournel. Some of them welcome visitors, with regular tours of the chais, tastings and even museums. At others entry is strictly by invitation, and those invitations are hard to obtain.

Rosi Hanson

At Château Loudenne in 1980 they re-opened the cuisine des vendanges (harvest kitchen) which had previously fallen into disuse. It is a beautiful L-shaped dining-room with two large fireplaces. Gleaming, copper-covered basins (chaudrières) with decorative taps shaped like the head and neck of a goose are set in a blue-and-white tiled potager (the same word as is used for a kitchen garden but here it means a kind of simmering-stove. There are other nice examples at Château Figeac and Château Grand Mayne in St Emilion).

This is an outstanding example of an old method of cooking; under the copper basins are holes for the hot coals. It is still used for dishes that need long, slow simmering, such as jambon au foin (ham cooked with hay) or pot-au-feu. Potagers were also used for keeping soup and vegetables warm. The room is used during the harvest, as well as for dinners throughout the year. Since 2013 the château has new, Chinese owners.

Josette, cook here for 27 years, made use of the produce grown in the garden. Homemade redcurrant jelly and blackcurrant jam was made for the visiting customers' breakfasts and an unusual jam from figs, apples and grapes; an old fig tree grows at the entrance to the kitchen and another door gives onto the estate's vines.

There are jars of compôe de pommes for desserts; peaches are made into sorbets. Duck preserved in its own fat (confit de canard) and preserved duck livers (foies gras de canard) are more of her specialities and pintade aux figues and pintade aux raisins (guinea-fowl with figs or grapes) are favourite ways of using the abundant figs and grapes at harvest time.

TAKE AWAY LUNCH AT LYNCH-BAGES

In the kitchen at Château Lynch-Bages the cooks are cutting up 58 stuffed rabbits which have just come out of the oven ready for the pickers' lunch. A still-life of baskets has been arranged on a big counter under a small window. On closer inspection the baskets are all named. There are one or two old-fashioned looking, metal food containers. There is a sudden whirlwind of activity as the cooks fill the baskets with an assortment of plastic boxes - this is a three-course packed lunch. The window is opened and the pickers come to collect their baskets in relays and take them home to eat. These are locals, many work for the château all through the year and the lady handing out the baskets knows exactly which one belongs to whom, and who likes this and doesn't like that. After lunch the baskets are returned with clean boxes, ready for the evening meal.

Other harvesters - from many different countries and somehow communicating in a variety of languages - are eating the same menu in the refectory. The excellent rabbit is stuffed with pork, onion, garlic, parsley and eggs and is served with a smooth potato purée.

With 85 hectares producing around 35,000 cases, Lynch-Bages is a typical size for the properties here. But it is family-owned, by the Cazes. It was run for many years by the dynamic Jean-Michel Cazes, whose style is very different from most Médocains. Having had a successful career in business, he put the same energy into the family property.

The management of Lynch-Bages is now in the hands of Jean-Charles Cazes. The Château receives literally hundreds of visitors, journalists and camera-crews from all over the world each year; the huge PR operation runs with well-oiled efficiency combined with cosmopolitan friendliness.

CH. LYNCH-BAGES' RABBIT WITH A STUFFING OF PORK, PARSLEY & GARLIC

Le Lapin Farci

FOR 6 PEOPLE
1 large rabbit
butter

FOR THE STUFFING:
20 ml (2 dessertspoons) milk
125 g (4 oz) bread, crusts removed
1 onion
2 cloves garlic
a good handful of fresh parsley
300 g (10 oz) pure pork sausage-meat
2 eggs
salt and pepper

Preheat the oven to gas mark 6, 400°F, 200°C.

Rosi Hanson

To make the stuffing, warm the milk and soak the bread in it for 10 minutes. Meanwhile, peel and chop the onion and garlic finely. Chop the parsley. Mix with the sausage-meat in a large bowl. Add the milk and bread to this mixture, then incorporate the eggs, one at a time, Season.

Stuff the rabbit with this mixture. Sew up the opening.

Smear the rabbit with butter and roast in the preheated oven for approximately one hour. Baste once or twice during the cooking. If it looks as if it is getting dry, pour a little hot water into the bottom of the roasting pan. You may need to lower the heat half-way through.

Cut up the rabbit and serve, making sure everyone gets some of the stuffing.

ROAST GUINEA-FOWL WITH FIGS IN A CREAM SAUCE
Pintade aux Figues

FOR 3 - 4 PEOPLE
1 guinea-fowl including giblets (feeds 3, or possibly 4, depending on appetite and what other dishes are served),
butter
6-8 figs
beurre manié (a teaspoon of flour or corn flour with a teaspoon of butter worked into it)
150 ml (5 fl oz) crème fraîche

FOR THE STOCK:
giblets

1 glass white wine
300 ml (½ pint) water
1 onion
1 large carrot
1 stick of celery
1 leek
bouquet garni of parsley, thyme and bay leaf

Preheat the oven to gas mark 6, 400°F, 200°C.

Smear the outside of the guinea-fowl with butter and put a lump inside. Place upside down in a roasting tin and roast in the preheated oven for 20 minutes. Turn breast side up, baste with the juices and continue roasting for another 25 minutes.

Meanwhile, make the stock. Cut up all the vegetables and put them in a pan with the rest of the stock ingredients. Bring to the boil and simmer for about half an hour. Strain and taste. It may need to be reduced by fast boiling for about 5 minutes, to concentrate the flavour. Spoon off any fat.

When the guinea-fowl is cooked, remove from the oven and keep warm while finishing the sauce. Put the figs into the hot oven to warm through. Pour off any fat from the roasting tin, place the tin over a medium heat on top of the cooker and pour in some of the stock. Scrape the bottom of the tin with a wooden spoon to deglaze. Take the tin off the heat and carefully whisk the beurre manié into the stock and roasting juices and simmer to thicken slightly. When it is incorporated, add crème fraîche.* Keep tasting and decide what seasoning is needed. If you feel the sauce is too thick, add more stock.

Keep the sauce warm while you carve the guinea-fowl. Quarter the figs and arrange with the meat on a serving dish. Pour over the sauce and serve.

*If you prefer not to have a cream sauce, instead, at this point add a small glass of Madeira. Another variation is to replace the figs with grapes, same method.

VEAL STEW WITH ONIONS AND MUSHROOMS IN A CREAM & EGG SAUCE

Blanquette de Veau

The veal is cooked in stock with vegetables to make the basis of this lovely dish. The stock is then used to make a sauce, which is finished with cream and egg yolks. It is certainly not a difficult dish but there are several distinct steps and it will take about 2 ¼ hours to prepare and cook. It's a good example of the French repertoire of family dishes, coming a day or two after a chicken dish which will have produced a stock, and is not extravagant because it uses cheap cuts of meat, cooked slowly and with care. Only a small amount of cream is needed but, with the egg yolks, it is enough to make the sauce luxurious.

It just takes a little practice to move from one step to another smoothly and it gets easier each time it is made. It can be prepared ahead of time up to the point when the veal and onions are united with the sauce and mushrooms. One or two corners can be cut: it can be made without stock (better to use water than a stock cube) simply by increasing the number of vegetables and adding a glass of wine. Leave the vegetables with the veal in the final dish if you like. The mushrooms can be omitted: the dish is not so fine - but still good. It can also be made using lamb.

FOR 6 - 8 PEOPLE
1.5 kg (3 lb) boned stewing veal - a mixture of breast, short ribs from best end, shoulder, middle neck, scrag and knuckle. Very often the butcher will just offer 'stewing veal' which will probably be a mixture of these cuts. It is useful to have some gelatinous meat in the mixture.
1 onion
1 large carrot
2 celery stalks
bouquet garni of parsley, thyme and bay leaf
salt and whole black peppercorns
1 - 1.5 litres (2 - 2½ pints) chicken stock

TO FINISH:
about 20 very small onions (often sold for pickling) or 6 small onions
3 tablespoons butter
2 tablespoons flour
250 g (8 oz) small mushrooms, wiped clean
lemon juice
salt and pepper
150 ml (¼ pint) double cream
3 egg yolks

First cut the veal into cubes. Put them into a pan, cover amply with cold water and bring to the boil. Simmer for a few minutes - grey scum will rise to the surface. Drain into a colander and run under the cold tap to get rid of the scum. It may seem tempting to eliminate this small step, but it is important for the final flavour and appearance.

Now the veal is to be cooked with the stock and vegetables. Put the meat into a casserole with the onion, carrot, celery, bouquet garni, a pinch of salt, 6 black peppercorns and the stock, which should just cover the meat. Bring just to the boil, cover and simmer very slowly for about 1½ hours. Test after 1¼ hours by sticking a fork into the meat - it should feel tender without falling apart.

If you have been able to buy little onions, they must be peeled and cooked whole in some of the stock. Otherwise, peel and cut the onions in four. Take a ladleful out of the casserole and simmer them in a small pan for about 30 minutes.

Once the veal is cooked, drain it, keeping the stock ready to make the sauce. Rinse the casserole. Melt the butter in a pan and stir in the flour. When smoothly amalgamated, start adding the stock. You may not need all of it. The sauce should not be very thick and there should be enough to cover the veal when you return it to the pan. Simmer for a few minutes - if a skin forms on top, skim it off. Add the mushrooms and simmer for 10 minutes. Taste the sauce after this and add salt, pepper and lemon juice, as necessary. The lemon juice is important to balance the cream and egg yolks, so at this stage the sauce should taste quite lemony. Put the veal and the onions into the casserole, pour the sauce over them and bring back to simmering point. Meanwhile, whisk the egg yolks and cream together in a bowl. Take a ladleful of the sauce and beat into the egg and cream mixture. Pour it all into the casserole and mix with the rest of the sauce. It should only cook for a few more minutes and should not boil. The blanquette is usually served with boiled rice, noodles or steamed potatoes.

Two dishes using boiling fowl:

CHICKEN WITH RICE AND A CREAM SAUCE
Poule au Riz à la Crème

This comforting dish has much in common with a blanquette. Like the preceding dish, it is simmered slowly in stock with vegetables; some of the stock is used to make a sauce, to which you add cream and egg yolks, and some to cook the rice to serve with it.

FOR 6 PEOPLE
100 g (4 oz) unsmoked streaky bacon
1 boiling fowl including giblets, total weight
about 2 kg (4 lb)
2 onions, sliced
4 carrots, sliced
2.25 litres (4 pints) stock, either made
from the giblets and some veal bones, or saved from
another boiled chicken dish
bouquet garni of parsley, thyme and bay leaf
2 cloves garlic
375 g (12 oz) white long-grain rice
45g (1½ oz) butter
2 tablespoons plain flour
2 egg yolks
250 ml (8 fl oz) single cream
lemon juice

Lay the slices of bacon on the bottom of a large, heavy, oval casserole. Put in the chicken and surround with the onions and carrots. Cook over a moderate heat until the bacon fat melts - do not let it get so hot that it burns. Meanwhile, heat the stock in another pan. When the bacon is ready, add the hot stock, bouquet garni and garlic, cover and simmer gently for 2 ½ to 3 hours.

About 30 minutes before the chicken is ready, measure out 1 litre (1¾ pints) of stock from the casserole. Put 750 ml (1¼ pints) into a pan with the rice and 15 g (½ oz) of the butter and bring just to the boil. Turn down the heat. Cover with foil and a tight-fitting lid and cook gently on the lowest possible heat for about 25 minutes without lifting the lid. Turn off the heat and leave another 5 minutes before taking the lid off and turning out onto a dish.

Once the rice is simmering, start making the sauce. Melt the rest of the butter in a pan, stir in the flour and cook for 2 to 3 minutes, then gradually add the remaining 300 ml (½ pint) of warm stock. Stir over the heat for a few minutes as it thickens. Make sure it is smooth. Beat the egg yolks in a small bowl with a tablespoon of the cream. Add the rest of the cream to the sauce and let it simmer for about 5 minutes. Take a spoonful of the hot sauce and stir it into the egg mixture, then mix this into the sauce. Stir it for a few more minutes over the gentle heat, then taste for seasoning. It needs a squeeze of lemon to give it some acidity or it will be too blandly creamy.

Remove the chicken from the pot. Pour the remaining stock through a sieve and reserve, discarding the bacon and vegetables, for making soup. Carve the chicken and arrange on a dish with the sauce poured over. Serve the rice separately. Poule au riz is usually served without vegetables but is nice followed by a green salad with quite a sharp vinaigrette.

POACHED STUFFED CHICKEN
Poule au Bouillon Farcie or Poule au Pot

There are many versions of this good value but delicious dish which must have originated as a way to make a tough old bird tender. By stuffing it and simmering for a long time with many vegetables, it became a more interesting dish and fed more people. The stuffing usually incorporates the chicken liver, bread soaked in milk and some meat either in the form of ham or minced veal or pork.

FOR 6 PEOPLE
1 boiling fowl including giblets, total weight
about 2 kg (4 lb)

FOR THE STUFFING:
200 g (7 oz) white bread, crusts removed
a little milk
200 g (7 oz) minced veal or pork
1 thick slice of Parma or other raw ham
2 tablespoons chopped onion
approximately 1 tablespoon butter
2 cloves garlic, chopped,
the chicken liver, and the gizzard, if liked

1 tablespoon of chopped fresh parsley
1 teaspoon of dried thyme
salt and pepper
grated nutmeg
2 eggs

VEGETABLES FOR THE POT:
2 medium onions
4 medium carrots
2 turnips
2 sticks of celery
2 leeks
bouquet garni of parsley, thyme and bay leaf

To make the stuffing, soak the bread in milk for a few minutes, then squeeze fairly dry and put in a bowl large enough for all the rest of the stuffing ingredients. Add the minced meat. Chop the raw ham and add. Cook the onion in the butter slowly until soft, then add to the bowl with the garlic. Clean the chicken liver and chop it with the gizzard if used, and add. Add the herbs and seasoning. Finally add the two eggs and stir it all until well mixed.

Stuff the chicken with this mixture and sew up the opening so that the stuffing does not escape during the cooking. (Special large needles and fine string are sold for this purpose in kitchen equipment shops.) Put the chicken in a large flameproof pot with all the vegetables, peeled and roughly chopped, and the bouquet garni. Cover with water and bring to the boil. Any scum rising to the top should be skimmed off. Turn the heat down as low as possible, cover and simmer for about 3 hours - it is hard to be precise about a boiling fowl - you want the meat to be tender, just beginning to come off the bone easily, but not overcooked so that it becomes stringy. To serve, cut up the chicken and surround with the vegetables and stuffing.

As these vegetables have given all their goodness to the stock (which will make an excellent soup), some people remove the vegetables from the stock about 30 minutes before they judge the chicken to be ready and replace them with a fresh selection, including potatoes if liked. Little pickled gherkins can also be served with it.

The chicken can be served with rice that has been cooked in some of the stock.

People often complain that chickens are tasteless nowadays, but boiling fowl usually have lots of flavour, so it is worth trying to get one.

Rosi Hanson

BACON JOINT POACHED WITH VEGETABLES
Le Salé de Porc

An old-fashioned peasant dish that the French sigh over nostalgically, this uses an economic cut of pork, which is usually salted nowadays by the charcutier, but used to be salted at home.

Pork takes salting and/or smoking very well. The joint known as petit salé in France is a piece of breast or belly of pork. For this dish, you need to buy a mild-cure, unsmoked bacon joint. Incidentally, the French call bacon 'lard de poitrine' or just 'lard'. A rasher of bacon is 'une tranche de lard', not very often eaten fried or grilled as we do, although during the harvest in the Bordeaux region it is sometimes grilled over vine-shoots. What is known as 'bacon' does not correspond to our bacon at all. What we call lard, they call 'saindoux'. All this can cause confusion when shopping in France.

FOR 6 - 8 PEOPLE
1 kg (2 lb) of mild-cure green bacon in a piece
1 kg (2 lb) carrots
1 kg (2 lb) potatoes
2 medium turnips
1 stick of celery
1 cabbage, usually Savoy but other kinds will do
3 leeks
1 medium onion
2 cloves garlic
salt and pepper
French mustard, to serve

Cover the bacon joint with cold water in a big pot. Bring it to the boil. Skim if necessary. Simmer for 30 minutes.

Meanwhile, prepare the vegetables - peel the carrots, potatoes and turnips, wash the celery, trim the outside leaves from the cabbage and leeks and wash. Peel and coarsely chop the onion and garlic. Cut the cabbage into four, cut any very large potatoes in two. Add all the vegetables to the pot after the first half hour. Season with pepper - as the bacon has been salted you will be unlikely to need salt, check at the end. Bring back just to the boil and simmer very slowly for a further 2½ hours. Drain the meat and vegetables (taste the stock - if it is not too salty, it can be used for soup).

Skin the pork, slice and serve on a bed of the vegetables, with a pot of Dijon mustard on the table.

BACON JOINT WITH LENTILS
Petit Salé aux Lentilles

The bacon joint is boiled and served on a bed of lentils, which is an excellent combination. The best kind of lentils to use are small, round and dark, known as Puy; the green-brown, flatter kind are fine; orange ones are not, as they cook to a mush.

FOR 6 - 8 PEOPLE
1 k g (2 lb) mild-cure green bacon in one piece
2 - 3 shallots, peeled
bouquet garni of parsley, thyme and bay leaf
1 leek, cleaned and chopped
2 carrots, chopped
6 black peppercorns
500 g (1 lb) lentils, preferably Puy

Cover the bacon joint with cold water in a pan. Bring slowly to the boil, then simmer for 30 minutes. Drain and put the joint in fresh water to cover. Add the vegetables, bouquet garni and peppercorns. Bring to the boil and simmer slowly for about an hour.

Meanwhile, rinse the lentils then boil until soft but not disintegrating - this will probably take about 15 mins. Drain, stir in a knob of butter, then season with salt and pepper and a squeeze of lemon. Delicious, served with the slices of hot bacon joint arranged on top and mustard.

FRENCH COTTAGE PIE
Hachis Parmentier

You hear French people sighing over the memory of a good Hachis Parmentier although it is not a thing you often see on a menu in France. Families usually love it and it is a favourite dish for the harvesters. The dish takes its name from Antoine-Auguste Parmentier, an agronomist who, in the late eighteenth century, successfully encouraged the French to regard potatoes as a worthwhile food.

Hachis Parmentier cannot be made from fresh meat - well, of course it could be, but that would defeat the object. It is a dish to make when you have a sufficient quantity of well-flavoured left-over meat for your family. During the harvest it is most frequently made with left-over boiled beef from a pot-au-feu. This can be supplemented with any meal left from a roast, usually beef but it can be a mixture. It is impossible to give exact quantities but here is the method:-

Make a smooth and creamy potato purée with plenty of butter and milk. It should not be stiff and certainly not lumpy, and should be well-seasoned.

Mince the meat, then add to a pan in which some chopped onions have been softened in butter. Now add a good handful (or more depending on the amount of meat) of fresh parsley. Other fresh herbs could be used instead if available, otherwise use dried ones. Season well and moisten with some stock from the pot-au-feu or juices kept from the roast. It should not be sloppy, but neither should it be dry.

Take a gratin dish, butter it and spread half the purée over the bottom. Now spread the meat mixture over this. Spread the rest of the purée over the top. Dot with butter. Put it into the oven at about gas mark 4, 350°F, 180°C for approximately half an hour, until the whole is piping hot and the top is appetisingly brown with crunchy bits round the edge.

FIGS IN RED WINE
Figues au Vin Rouge

Wine-makers often have to open several bottles at a time so that customers can taste their range of wines in the different vintages; the remains of the bottles are generally used to top up barrels. Sometimes they find their way into the family's vinegar barrel or into the kitchen, where inspired combinations may evolve. Figs in red wine is one such partnership…

It only takes a few minutes to prepare - and these figs improve if made the day before they are to be eaten.

FOR 6 - 8 PEOPLE
24 ripe figs, wiped clean
500 ml (15fl oz) red wine
125 g (4 oz) caster sugar
3 or 4 drops vanilla essence
1 pinch of ground allspice or a
mixture of nutmeg, cloves and
cinnamon or ginger

Quarter the figs without cutting right through the skin - just open them up. Arrange them in one layer in a flameproof casserole.

In another pan, bring the wine to the boil with the sugar, vanilla essence and spice, then pour over the figs. Simmer for 10 minutes. Put aside to cool.

Lift out the figs and arrange in bowls, then pour over some of the wine. Serve chilled.

PEACHES IN RED WINE
Pêches au Vin Rouge

1st VERSION FOR 6 PEOPLE:
approximately 1 kg (2 lb) ripe peaches
(at least one peach per person)
1 bottle red wine
1 tablespoon kirsch, optional
200 g (7 oz) caster sugar

Pour boiling water over the peaches, leave for 5 minutes, then plunge them into cold water and peel them. Cut them in half and take out the stones. Slice evenly. Marinade the peaches overnight in the wine, kirsch and sugar. That is all. The kirsch is a refinement; it can be made without it or you could experiment with other fruit brandies.

2nd VERSION:

This takes the same ingredients but with small peaches, if possible. Peel the peaches as before, but leave them whole. Marinate overnight as for the first version. The next day poach them in the marinade for about ten minutes, then lift them out and drain. Reduce the marinade by fast boiling by about a quarter, until it is just slightly syrupy. Pour over the peaches and cool. This dish is best if made the previous day and kept in the fridge.

PEACHES AND PRUNES SIMMERED IN SPICED WINE
Pêches des Vignes et Pruneaux d'Agen au Vin Rouge

FOR 6-8 PEOPLE
2 kg (4 lb) small peaches (1-2 per person depending on size)
twice as many prunes as peaches
1 bottle red wine
250 g (8 oz) caster sugar
a stick of cinnamon
12 peppercorns
12 coriander seeds

Pour boiling water over the peaches, leave for 5 minutes, then plunge them into cold water and peel them. (It is not absolutely necessary to do this - some people leave the skins on.) Cut them in half and remove the stones. You should now have an equal quantity of peach halves and prunes. Put the wine, sugar and spices into an enamelled pan and bring to the boil. Add the peaches and prunes and simmer until the fruit are cooked, about 15 to 20 minutes - longer if they were under-ripe. Put aside to cool, then chill in the fridge overnight. Place a prune in each peach half and arrange the fruit in a bowl. Sieve the wine to remove the spices and pour it over the fruit.

SIMPLE APPLE COMPÔTE
Compôte de Pommes

Take good eating apples, peel, core and slice them into an enamelled cast-iron casserole, squeezing lemon juice over the slices. Sprinkle them with vanilla-flavoured sugar, cover and simmer over a low heat or in a low temperature oven. If you are worried that they will catch or burn on the bottom of the pan, add 1 tablespoon of water, but this is really unnecessary if they cook slowly enough. They should be ready in about half an hour, depending on the variety used and how much you want the fruit to retain the shape of its slices. The apples are at their best served warm or hot. They can be accompanied by slices of gâteau au vin blanc, with little biscuits, or with the following recipe.

LITTLE CUSTARD POTS
Oeufs au Lait

These individual baked custards can easily be made in quantity, as long as you have a large oven and enough little Pyrex or other ovenproof ramekins, so they are a frequent harvest dessert. They may be served as an accompaniment to a compôte, or on their own with biscuits. The changes may be rung by flavouring them with vanilla, grated lemon peel, chocolate or coffee.

FOR 6 PEOPLE
For 6 ramekins (capacity about 125 ml/4fl oz)
2 medium eggs
300 ml (½ pint) milk
15 g (½ oz) caster sugar
4 drops vanilla essence
nutmeg
butter for greasing

Optional nutmeg for grating on top
Preheat the oven to gas mark 2, 300°F, 150°C.

Preheat the oven to gas mark 2, 300°F, 150°C.

Break the eggs into a bowl. Lightly beat them with a fork. Add the milk, sugar and vanilla and stir to mix well.

Butter the ramekins. Strain the mixture through a sieve into a jug. Fill the ramekins with the mixture. Arrange them in a roasting tin; pour in cold water to reach half-way up the ramekins. Bake in the preheated oven for 20 to 30 minutes. If they cook too long or too fast they will form a tough skin on top and/or curdle. Check after 20 minutes - give a ramekin a little nudge to see if it has set. Grate a little nutmeg on top.

HOT SPICED WINE
Vin Chaud aux Epices

In cold vintages, this is served at Haut Sarpe to warm up the pickers when they get back from the vines. Some people like to add a dash of fruit brandy, or marc (brandy distilled from the skins and pips after the harvest). In the Loire local, sweetish, white vin doux is sometimes used for this (cut down on the added sugar)

FOR 6 - 8 PEOPLE
1 bottle of an every-day drinking red wine
nothing too subtle
about 1 tablespoon lemon juice
1 stick of cinnamon
1 clove
1 vanilla pod
a pinch of grated nutmeg,
125 g (4 oz) caster sugar or if liked,
a light brown sugar

Simply place all the ingredients in a pan, bring slowly to the boil, then serve straightaway.

LOIRE

The valley of the great river Loire is well known for its soft beautiful light, beloved by painters, and for its many fine châteaux and gardens, as well as for its vineyards. What must strike anyone in search of those vineyards is the great distance – 400 km from the mouth of the Loire to Sancerre - you must drive if you wish to visit them all. But it is a journey well worth making, with beautiful changing scenery as you cross and re-cross the meandering river and its many tributaries, and opportunities to visit the markets of the region.

In terms of wine, the area just south-east of the mouth of the Loire is known as Muscadet. Nearby Nantes is the town which has given its name to the sauce beurre Nantais, also known as beurre blanc, which often accompanies the alose (the seawater shad which spawns in rivers), sandre (the freshwater pike-perch), or brochet (pike) fished in the river Loire. The Muscadet is a large vineyard area, producing mainly white wine which is from one grape type, now called the Muscadet grape but originating in Burgundy where it was known as the Melon de Bourgogne. This produces the crisp white wine which is so often served in France with seafood, particularly oysters, mussels and crabs. That of Sèvre et Maine has the highest reputation and the best wines are bottled straight from the vat, sur lies (unfiltered), and have a refreshing little tingle on the tongue.

Moving eastwards up-river, we come to the town of Angers (which also lays claim to the beurre blanc - and it is true that the shallots which are a vital ingredient are grown around here). Red, rosé and white wines, both dry and sweet, are all made in the Anjou. The white grape here is the Chenin Blanc, which in Savennières produces an unusual dry white as well as a sweet wine.

South of the river - so many times do you find yourself crossing a bridge here it is sometimes hard to remember which bank of the river you are on - the best dessert wines of the Loire are produced in Quarts de Chaume, Côteaux du Layon and Bonnezeaux. It is the local habit to drink these rich, sweet wines with the great pork dishes and, in particular, the wide range of charcuterie for which the region is renowned.

Towards Tours one finds the red wine Saumur Champigny, which is deliciously fruity when drunk young. It is made from the Cabernet Franc which is the grape widely planted in Bordeaux around St Emilion. Chinon and Bourgueil are the two Loire red wines most often considered for ageing; production is tiny, which accounts for the fact that they were relatively unknown until recently.

Along this stretch of the river are some of the great châteaux and early churches for which the Loire is famed. In a number of villages the houses seem to have been grafted onto cliffs. Numerous caves in these cliffs provide perfect natural conditions for the cultivation of mushrooms: there is even a little museum of mushroom culture near Saumur.

From Saumur up to Vouvray, sparkling white wine is made using the champagne method (méthode champenoise) and sold as Crémant de Loire. Dry, medium-dry and sweet white wines of the area are also made. These sweeter wines (on the label they may be described as doux), while not finding an appreciative market very often in the U.K. or U.S.A., nevertheless seem in keeping with the lush scenery of the Loire river and go well with some of the local dishes. Although it may seem strange to marry a sweet wine with fish, it can balance the acidity of the beurre blanc which is the usual accompaniment to the whole poached fish served in the restaurants along the banks of the river. A more obvious combination is made of these wines and the wonderful fruit of the area used in open tarts.

For many, the most important wine-growing area of the Loire valley is Sancerre and its neighbour, Pouilly Fumé (not to be confused with Pouilly Fuisse in Burgundy's Maconnais area). Here the Sauvignon Blanc grape is planted on gently sloping hillsides, (although some can be vertiginous, like the Monts Damnés in Chavignol), producing a white wine combining qualities of pungent fruitiness with acidity, which makes it ideal as an appetite-awakening aperitif. Alongside the vineyards are the goat farms which produce the celebrated crottins de Chavignol - delicious little cheeses which can be eaten fresh or slightly aged. The wines have become quite high-priced, but not far away are the villages of Ménétou-Salon, Quincy and Reuilly where the Sauvignon Blanc grape gives wines which are cheaper and well worth exploring.

Although vines have become important to the economy of the Loire, it was not always so. This was, and to quite a large extent still is, an area of mixed farming. In the Muscadet, where real poverty was experienced by smallholders until well after the last war, the production of linen was as important, if not more so, than wine.

That mixed farming continues is one of the pleasures of travelling in the Loire. One may round a corner in the high plâteau of the Anjou to find a brightly-coloured strip of flowers being harvested for market. One passes through vineyards, then maize, asparagus, or arable land. Here fermes-auberges (farms serving meals and sometimes providing simple accommodation) which are often booked by wine-growers for their end of harvest celebrations, still exist serving excellent local food in basic but friendly surroundings.

Recipes from the French Wine Harvest

LINEN AND MUSCADET - PRE-WAR LIFE IN THE VINES

Listening to the rumbustious, splendidly moustachioed Jean-Yves Secher discussing the harvest dishes of his childhood with his wife and mother is like being buffeted by a strong but warm wind. There are fierce arguments about details - amicably resolved - and strongly held views about social change, and much laughter too.

This family, who make Muscadet de Sèvre et Maine Clos des Bourguignons (so-called because it was one of the original vineyards planted with Melon de Bourgogne vines in the eighteenth century), used to lodge and feed forty pickers, but since 1984 they have used a picking machine. For Jean-Yves it was the new laws raising the basic agricultural wage, introduced in 1968, which proved a turning point. Until then little had changed in this rural community.

The picture of the past that emerged was of a hard life, with few luxuries or entertainments. Here vines and flax, liking the same kind of soil, were both cultivated. Most vignerons kept a pig, one or two cows and some hens. There were few shops, just the grocer for essentials: little was eaten that was not grown or raised on the farm. Mme Secher senior remembered harvest food before the war: café-au-lait, bread and butter first thing, then a mid-day meal, which was carried up to the vines in baskets on the back and consisted of a dish of beans, or a salad, a home-reared chicken, duck or rabbit and possibly a piece of Camembert, although cheese was generally considered to be a luxury at that time. In the evening there would be a bowl of soup - probably soupe aux choux (cabbage soup), or soupe au pain (bread soup, see below) followed by fruit, pêches des vignes, the little peaches from the trees often planted in the vineyards, or apples or pears from the orchard.

This is their recipe for la pannade - bread soup (also known locally as la mittonée):

Water, bread, butter, salt, sometimes milk, are the ingredients of this homely soup. The bread and water are gently simmered until the bread is broken down ('until it is like glue,' said one member of the Secher family), then a lump of butter, salt and a little milk is added. This is a thick concoction - Jean-Yves said 'the spoon stands up in it,' but this was hotly disputed by other members of the family. The kind of bread used came from the big loaves of country bread which could weigh three kilos (six pounds) - they were made with unrefined flour and had a lot more goodness and fibre in them than most modern French bread. The soup was also eaten in the mornings at breakfast by Mme Secher's grandparents before they went into the vines.

Les trempinettes (although sweet, this was eaten as a first course - it seems closely related to the kind of possets and caudles popular in eighteenth-century Britain) as told by the Secher family:

'You put sugar in a tureen and pour in some hot water. Then you add toast, cut up small, and then some wine, red or white as you please and stir gently. You put in as much sugar as is to your taste, and as many litres of wine as you like - and a glass of eau de vie if you like. If you like a lot of sugar then you need lots of wine! You eat it with a spoon, like a soup. It must be freshly made.'

Here in the Loire, the pig supplies the ingredients for many of the best dishes and it was usual to kill one before the harvest. Hams were cured; sausages made, some to be smoked in the chimney; bacon joints were salted in charniers (large earthenware salting pots), later to be soaked in fresh water, boiled with herbs for 1½ hours and eaten cold in slices; rillons, richauds, rillauds and rillots are all alternative names for the same dish which is rather confusing, made from the unsalted belly of pork; rillettes made similarly but without the extra chunks of pork; and boulettes, another economical dish, were made, sometimes with pork or with a mixture of pork and rabbit.

At the Domaine aux Moines in Savennières, a different, calmer atmosphere prevails. A small country road winds out of the quiet little town of Savennières up into the steeper vineyards. The Loire can be glimpsed in the distance. At the time of the harvest, the glowing, autumnal reds of the Virginia creeper which covers the old vat-house and farm buildings make a beautiful sight. Tiny pink cyclamen are in flower at the foot of the walls and under trees which surround this lovely house. A terrace running the length of the house gives onto a formal garden which, in 1930, was restored and laid out as it was when monks cultivated the vines here in the Middle Ages.

Mme Laroche has been handing over to her daughter in recent years. When I first visited, this estate was remarkable for the way the use of modern aids, such as a freezer, was combined with a respect for old standards. Hens were kept, a kitchen garden provided vegetables and fruit, a pig was reared and killed in good time for the harvest.

As much as possible was done ahead of time, because during the harvest Mme Laroche was busy in the vines supervising the picking, to-ing and fro-ing in an old truck between vines, vat-house and kitchen, with not much time to cook. Joints of pork to roast were prepared and frozen, ready to be cooked and served to her small team of about ten pickers – the Laroche children were joined by other students and her two permanent cellar-workers; rillettes and terrines were made and, in the traditional way, nothing of the pig was wasted.

The domaine mainly makes dry white wine from its nine hectares, although one small parcel of vines across the road from the house is planted with the Cabernet grape to make an excellent and rare red Savennieres. Despite being a small estate, the harvest takes three weeks, for they pass twice or sometimes three times through the same vineyards, selecting and picking the grapes as they reach ripeness.

Favourite dishes included those roasts of pork, the first week cooked slowly with onions, tomatoes and potatoes and, to ring the changes later in the vendanges, spread with mustard, wrapped in pates feuilletés and accompanied by whole garlic cloves baked in their skins and plenty of frîtes.

Boudins noirs (black puddings) were made - these darkly gleaming coils are perhaps an acquired taste, but there are those for whom they are a great gastronomic treat despite their humble, not to say frugal, origins. A local version, known as la gogue is unusual in that it contains many green vegetables - chard, lettuces and leeks amongst them - and is very large. At the Domaine aux Moines the boudins were served in the traditional French way, sliced and grilled, accompanied by sweet apples, sliced and tossed in butter, and a smooth, creamy purée of potatoes.

Chickens were either roasted plainly, or cut up and sautéed in butter with mustard, lemon juice and curry powder and served with rice. Poulet Angevine, a local dish, was also served. Mme Laroche always roasted a turkey at least once during the harvest, serving the white meat at lunch and using the carcass with the brown meat to make a good stock to be served with lots of vegetables cooked in it, for an evening soup.

For lapin à la moutarde, a rabbit cut in pieces is sautéed, then coated with mustard; a little cognac is poured over and flamed, and the dish is simmered in the oven. Just before serving a pot of crème fraîche is added to the cooking juices to make a sauce.

The Laroches have an orchard full of fruit trees and most of their desserts made good use of this. They always have a glut of pears at the time of the harvest and hardly a day went by without at least one pear tart being eaten, Mme Laroche remembered.

ONION SOUP FOR BREAKFAST IN THE ANJOU

Vignerons in Anjou and Touraine more often than not find themselves harvesting late in October - and October in the vines can be cold. Further south, with earlier harvests, pickers are usually dressed in T-shirts, and in some hot years bikinis and bare torsos are de rigueur amongst the rows. But here oilskins and heavy jerseys are more suitable as early morning temperatures come close to freezing. A good breakfast is called for, thinks the Biotteau family.

Their large, well-placed house commands a beautiful view over the surrounding countryside. It has substantial farm buildings, vat-house and kitchen garden. Their own produce - pigs, hens, ducks, guinea-fowl, rabbits, vegetables and fruit - is used for the harvest meals. A well-equipped modern refectory and kitchens have been built to serve the hundred or so pickers in the autumn and are available for hire throughout the year for weddings or other receptions.

The copious breakfast served to put their harvesters in good heart on a cold, raw morning very often starts with an onion soup. Homemade rillettes also keep the cold out, and so do côtes de porc, a piece of pork loin, roasted in the oven, and eaten cold with mustard. There is plenty of fresh bread and homemade butter to go with the charcuterie. Tartines des graisses are popular; these are slices of the fattier belly of pork joint, roasted and when cold, sliced, spread with mustard and eaten on bread. If the morning is really chilly, hot sugared wine is sent up to the vineyards.

Drawing on the farm's resources, the Domaine Biotteau serve plenty of vegetable soups, and salads of beetroot, grated raw carrot and tomatoes make an hors d'oeuvre with homemade pâtés. There are four ladies at work in the kitchen, including the Biotteau's daughters and daughters-in-law, making pâtés and terrines and preparing the farm's poultry and other produce. Catherine Biotteau, who has married into another local wine-making family, the Richous, fondly recalls her childhood memories of the communal life lived at the time of the harvest and the feeling of working together.

At mid-day there is always a meat dish - beefsteak with frîtes, pork chops with sauté potatoes, beef simmered in wine, various ragoûts or coq au vin using their own poultry. Boudins noirs are sliced and grilled, but here they are often accompanied by a dish of semi-dried haricot beans - called les grenots locally. These need to be shelled, then simmered in water with an onion and bouquet garni for about an hour until tender and served with 'a good salad of endive with garlic,' according to Mme Biotteau.

Rosi Hanson

In every harvest cook's mind some dishes are for midday and others for evening - it seems to be an unwritten rule. In general, evening meals are lighter on the digestion and there is more likely to be a dessert. One of the Biotteau's supper dishes for the pickers is made from pig's liver. It is both simple and economical. The liver is sliced and browned in a little butter in a frying pan, then lifted out so that a sauce can be made in the same pan. This uses lots of finely chopped onions, or shallots if available. Adding more butter if necessary, they are cooked until soft, a little flour is added to the pan and some vin doux (local sweet white wine) to make enough sauce to cover the slices of liver which are now put back in the pan, and simmered for 30 minutes. This is 'liver and onions' the French way.

Desserts in the evening often consist of a compôte of apples or other fruit with a gâteau au vin blanc. Sometimes pears baked whole in the oven are served. This is a simple idea for making good use of cooking pears or windfall fruit. It takes no preparation except to put the clean, unpeeled fruit on a baking tray and into a medium oven. They emerge with all their juices intact about an hour later (sooner if smaller).

OLD FRIENDS AND FEASTING CHEZ COTAT IN CHAVIGNOL

The harvest at this small (they only need about a dozen pickers) but distinguished estate in Chavignol, near Sancerre, is always done by volunteers, friends from M. Cotat's army days - a kind of mini regimental reunion. When you meet Mme Cotat it is easy to understand why these faithful friends continue to take their holidays working for nothing in some of the steepest vineyards in the area, and bring their sons and nephews too. For Mme Cotat looks like a lady who loves to cook. Not that she is large, but in talking of recipes her eyes light up, she becomes animated - it is a subject of passionate interest. For this group she pulls out all the gastronomic stops. Round this table there is friendship and feasting and in the cellars, serious tasting to be done.

When they come in from the vines, the Cotat's band of volunteers are revived by going straight down into the cellars for a glass, or two, or four, of wine from the barrel. They can confidently expect to sit down afterwards to an excellent meal of some favourite dishes, such as a well-seasoned salad of potatoes and herring fillets, coq au vin flamed in marc (brandy distilled from the grape must left after the harvest) and simmered in Sancerre, followed by cheese and a dessert of caramelised gâteau de rhubarbe. There are ragouts of mutton or rabbit, or stuffed tomatoes; an ox tongue is cooked like a pot-au-feu, slowly with lots of vegetables, and served with a Madeira sauce - another favourite. On Sundays the lunch starts with a spinach tart followed by a good shoulder of mutton which has been marinated in white wine, oil and herbs, larded with many slivers of garlic, then spit-roasted over an open fire.

A street away, still in the pretty little village of Chavignol, the ladies of the Bourgeois family went on strike. This is a large and well-known estate, making Sancerre and using between 50 and 70 pickers. In 1990 Mme Bourgeois announced that she and her helper were exhausted after years of cooking for the harvest - a new system must be found! Now most of the pickers are local people who go home after work, and these ladies, who look after customers in the attractive tasting-room and in the family shop on the main street, only cook in the evenings. There are still about fifteen pickers to be lodged and fed, as well as the vat-house workers.

Lapin au Sancerre is one of the best dishes here. The jointed rabbit is browned and simmered slowly in white wine with mushrooms for two hours, then potatoes are added in a layer on top about twenty minutes before serving. All the usual plats mijotés - the long-cooking stews - which form the backbone of harvest cooking are in the Bourgeois repertoire as well as des grillades - grilled meat dishes.

Fruit compôtes go well with the sweet biscuits made and sold in the shops here and known as croquets de Sancerre, or lichous de Sancerre, or with a gâteau au vin blanc.

THE BIOTTEAU'S ONION SOUP
Soupe à L'Oignon

This is certainly not an elegant party soup! It has a soothing, almost medicinal quality (excellent if you are suffering from a cold).

FOR 6 PEOPLE
2 large onions
approximately 60 g (2 oz) butter
approximately 2 teaspoons plain flour
1 - 1½ litres (1¾ - 2½ pints) water
freshly ground black pepper

Peel and chop the onions finely. Brown them in the butter in a heavy-based pan. They must be well-browned, 'not burnt but almost,' says Mme Biotteau. In practice this means cooking them quite briskly, but not frying them to a crisp, for about 10 to 15 minutes, stirring from time to time. The onions begin to caramelize. This is important to give flavour, because no stock is being used. Stir in enough flour to be absorbed by the buttery juices to make a roux. This is the moment to start adding the water, a little at first to avoid making the mixture lumpy, then the rest. Bring back to the boil and leave to simmer for about 10 minutes. Season the soup well with plenty of pepper.

As can be seen, this is a very simple soup. The Biotteau family sometimes add a little of their own vin doux.

Rosi Hanson

SPINACH, CREAM & CHEESE TART
Tarte aux Epinards

FOR 6 - 8 PEOPLE
FOR THE PASTRY:
250g (8 oz) plain flour
a pinch of salt
150 g (5 oz) soft butter
1 egg yolk
3 - 4 tablespoons cold water

FOR THE FILLING:
750g (1½ lb) fresh spinach, or 375g (12 oz) chopped,
frozen spinach
2 tablespoons butter
1 large onion, peeled and finely chopped
salt and freshly ground black pepper
250 g (8 oz) fromage blanc or fromage frais
(you can use a low fat one)
3 eggs, lightly beaten
60 g (2 oz) freshly grated Parmesan cheese,
150 g (5 oz) double cream
pinch of grated nutmeg

Preheat the oven to gas mark 4, 350°F, 180°C. Make the pastry in the usual way; use to line an 28 cm (11 in) tart tin. Bake blind for 15 minutes in the pre-heated oven.

Wash the fresh spinach and discard the stems. Blanch for five minutes in a big pan of boiling water. Drain, cool and squeeze dry with your hands. Chop roughly. If you are using frozen spinach you can omit this step and go straight to the next: melt the butter in a frying pan and cook the onion until soft. Add the spinach and let it cook in the butter for about 5 minutes, stirring to make sure it does not burn on the bottom. Add salt and pepper. Drain away any water which remains.

Off the heat, add the fromage blanc, the beaten eggs, Parmesan, cream and nutmeg. Mix all together and pour into the pastry case, spreading it evenly. Bake in the oven at the same temperature as before for 30 minutes, or until the pastry is browned and the filling has set. The top should brown but the consistency of the filling should be moist. Serve hot, warm or cold – it is delicious all ways!

GRATIN OF HARD-BOILED EGGS
Oeufs durs au gratin

This is a good dish to cook when you already have the oven on for roasting or baking. They may sound old-fashioned but they make a really nice, quick, first course or light lunch.

FOR 6 PEOPLE
7 eggs
1 tablespoon thick cream (crème fraîche if possible)
1 tablespoon grated Gruyère,
1 tablespoon chopped parsley
salt and freshly ground pepper

Preheat the oven to gas mark 6, 400°F, 200°C.

Put six of the eggs into a pan with enough cold water to cover. Bring them to the boil, simmer for 5 mins., turn off and leave for 5 more mins. Plunge the eggs into cold water and leave to cool. Shell and cut the eggs in half lengthwise. Scoop out the yolks into a bowl, mash with a fork. Lightly beat the remaining egg and add to the bowl together with the crème fraîche, Gruyère, parsley and seasoning. Spoon the quite liquid mixture into the eggs until they overflow, and put them in a lightly oiled gratin dish. You can do this ahead of time.
They now need a final five minutes in the top of a hottish oven or under a grill to melt the cheese and to brown. The trick is to get them really hot without overcooking.

POTTED PORK
Rillettes

Large bowls of this soft, melting kind of potted pork or pâté are in every charcuterie in the Loire. A fine example of the French talent for turning cheap ingredients into something delicious, it is easy to make at home.

FOR 8 PEOPLE
1 kg (2 lb) belly or neck of pork, rind and
bones removed
500 g (1 lb) pork back-fat
1 clove garlic
bouquet garni of parsley, thyme and bay leaf
salt and freshly ground black pepper

Cut the meat into short strips about the width of a finger. Cut up the back-fat coarsely. Put all into an ovenproof casserole with the garlic, herbs, salt and pepper and enough water just to cover the bottom of the pan. Cover and cook in a very slow oven - gas mark ½, 250°F, 120°C - for about four hours.

It cannot be said to look very appetising at this stage. The next step is to drain off the fat and keep it. Throw away the bouquet garni. Pound the meat in a pestle and mortar for a few minutes. The meat is soft and the job is easy. Resist the temptation to use a food processor - it ruins the texture which should not be that of a smooth paste. Finally, take two forks, one in each hand, and pull the pork into shreds. You end up with a pale mushroomy-pinky-brown mass of meat marbled with deeper pink streaks. Taste for seasoning and adjust if necessary - rillettes should not be bland.

Traditional rillette pots are like rather thick, salt-glazed, earthenware mugs, but any earthenware or china pot or bowl will do. Whatever you choose, pile the mixture into it without pressing it down into a compact paste. It is local practice to pour the reserved melted fat over the top.

Rillettes will keep for 2 to 3 weeks in a cool larder or fridge sealed by the fat (which is there to preserve rather than be eaten) and covered with foil. Remember to take them out of the fridge in good time before serving, so that they are soft, to spread on fresh bread and enjoy with a glass of Vouvray or other fruity Loire wine.

To make this dish with rabbit, use 250 g (8 oz) of rabbit to 750 g (1½ lb) of pork and cook with the other ingredients as for the pork.

For 'Rillons', add an extra half kilo (1 lb) of belly of pork, cut into roughly 5 cm (2 in) chunks, to the pork and fat of the original recipe. Cook as before. When you come to drain the fat off and before pounding the meat, extract these chunks and let them brown in a hotter oven. Eat them hot with a purée of potatoes, or cold as part of an hors d'oeuvre, (this is a close cousin of pork scratchings!)- either way with plenty of mustard.

MME LAROCHE'S PORK TERRINE

FOR 12 SERVINGS
500 g (1 lb) belly of pork, boned, rind removed
1 kg (2 lb) lean pork
6 allspice berries
1 egg, beaten
2 tablespoons cognac
150 ml (5fl oz) dry white wine
salt and freshly ground black pepper
caul fat, back-fat or slices of streaky bacon
to cover the terrine
bay leaf, optional

Preheat the oven to gas mark 4, 350°F, 180°C.

Mince the meat coarsely or ask your butcher to do it for you. The belly of pork should give enough fat to keep the terrine moist. Grind the allspice. Mix all the ingredients, apart from the fat or bacon, together in a bowl, making sure that the egg, cognac and wine are blended into the whole mixture. Season well.

Pack the mixture into a terrine, capacity about 1 litre (1¾ pints). You could use an earthenware or enamelled cast-iron terrine, or a meat-loaf tin which, if it has no lid, you will need to cover with two layers of foil. Caul fat, that thin lacy-looking fat, should be spread over the top. It is often difficult to obtain; if so, use either thinly cut strips of back-fat or streaky green bacon instead, although the latter will give a rather bacon-y flavour to the juices. The point is to use something that will help to keep the terrine moist. Put a bay leaf on top as a garnish, if liked.

Bake, with the lid on, in the preheated oven, for about 1½ hours. About 20 minutes before the end remove the lid and the covering fat, so that the top may brown a little.

Remove from the oven. Cover with a piece of foil or greaseproof paper, weight - you can use one or two cans of food if you have no measuring weights - and leave to cool. Once cold, remove the weights. It will improve if kept for a day or two before being broached and will keep about a week in the fridge. Any surplus fat will have solidified on top and can be easily removed.

Slice and eat with gherkins and some of the juices that have set to a jelly round the terrine.

BUTTER AND SHALLOT SAUCE FROM THE LOIRE
to go with a poached fish - Beurre Blanc

In the Loire valley you can eat this sauce with the local fish in little restaurants alongside the river. Here we are rarely able to get the same varieties, but it goes perfectly with salmon, or with white fish such as turbot or halibut, as well as giving a boost to cheaper varieties if you so wish. If you do have any left over, a small spoonful stirred into scrambled eggs as they finish cooking is rather good. Quantities are for 10. It is rare to have too much of this delicious sauce, so even if you are a smaller party it is worth making a lot.

10 small shallots
10 tablespoons good quality
white wine vinegar
10 tablespoons Muscadet
(Use the rest of the bottle to drink with the fish)
approximately 400 g (14 oz) unsalted butter, chilled

There are two stages to this sauce, neither of which take long, nor are they difficult. The first step is to prepare a good foundation.

Take the shallots and peel them. Use a sharp cook's knife and chop them very finely. Put them into a heavy enamelled pan, or tinned copper pan, with the wine and vinegar. The object of this exercise is to cook the shallots until they are soft, at the same time reducing the liquid by boiling without a lid until you are left with very little moisture in the bottom of the pan. The shallots must 'give up their oil' in this process. It is hard to be precise about the time this will take - 10 to 15 minutes perhaps.

You could put the pan aside at this stage, as long as the shallots are kept warm. The second stage must be carried out just before serving.

Have the butter ready, cut up into chunks of about 30 g (1 oz) each, and keep it cool until you need it. About 10 minutes before you are ready to serve the fish, put the pan back over a very low heat and start adding the chunks of butter, whisking them in one by one. The heat must not be so great that the butter starts to melt, so be ready to move the pan off the heat from time to time. Instead of melting, the butter must do what the French call 'mounting' (monter is the verb); if you have not seen this happen it is rather hard to visualise, but it is easy to do as long as the pan never gets too hot - better to have it too cool and go very slowly. Some people prefer to put the shallots and reduction into a bowl over a pan of simmering water i.e. a bain-marie – it is a safe way to make sure the butter does not melt. You should end up with a sauce the texture of thick cream. It is very delicious.

SALAD OF POTATOES AND SMOKED HERRING FILLETS
Salade de Pommes de Terre et Harengs Fumés

FOR 6 PEOPLE AS A FIRST COURSE
1 kg (2 lb) small waxy-fleshed potatoes
salt and freshly ground black pepper
1 medium onion
1 can or vacuum pack smoked herring fillets (about 200 gr/ 7 oz)
handful of fresh parsley

FOR THE VINAIGRETTE:
wine vinegar
walnut oil
groundnut oil

Wash the potatoes and boil in salted water. They should remain firm but cooked through.

While they are cooking, make the vinaigrette. One tablespoon of vinegar to three of oil is a fairly standard proportion for this kind of thing, but it is a matter of taste. It is usually more vinegary than a dressing for a green salad. The proportion of oils used would probably be two tablespoons of the cheaper groundnut oil to one of the expensive walnut oil.

Drain the potatoes and allow to cool until you can handle them. Peel them. Put them, the bigger ones cut in two, into a salad bowl. Pour over the vinaigrette and toss the potatoes in it while they are warm. Add salt and plenty of pepper.

Peel the onion and chop it finely. Mix it with the potatoes.

Drain any liquid from the herring fillets, cut them into smallish pieces and mix with the potatoes.

Wash, dry and finely chop the parsley, then add to the bowl. This salad rather needs the bright green as the colours are dull. It can be served while the potatoes are still warm, or left to absorb more of the flavours of the vinaigrette and served at room temperature.

The smoked herring fillets are available in most French supermarkets, but if you cannot get them there are other versions: kipper fillets (preferably oak-smoked) work well. Hard-boiled eggs and tinned anchovies make another good partnership with the potatoes.

Chopped shallots or red onions can be added - there should be plenty of them in proportion to the other ingredients.

BOULETTES DE PORC FROM THE SECHERS' KITCHEN

These are meatballs, or sausages without skin, made from fresh pork. Their cooking time is flexible, so they make a quick and easy lunch dish.

FOR 4 - 6 PEOPLE
1 onion
a good handful of fresh parsley
a little fresh or dried thyme
500 g (1 lb) minced pork, a mixture of lean and fat
salt and freshly ground pepper
plain flour
approximately 250 ml (8 fl oz) wine, optional

Preheat the oven to gas mark 4, 350°F, 180°C.

Peel and chop the onion finely. Chop the fresh parsley and thyme. Mix onions and herbs with the pork in a bowl. Season with salt and pepper. Take a tablespoonful of the mixture and squeeze it into a ball with your hands, then roll it in flour. Put aside until all the mixture is used.

Arrange the meatballs in an ovenproof casserole (an earthenware gratin dish could be used) and add a little water, or if you have an opened bottle, some wine, just to cover the bottom. Bake them in the preheated oven. Their cooking time can vary to fit your schedule, but allow 45 minutes to 1 hour in a medium oven (or longer at a lower heat if it suits you), just making sure they do not dry up, especially if you are using an open dish, by adding a little liquid and if necessary covering with foil. If you use a casserole you can put the lid on for most of the cooking and take the lid off and raise the heat to brown them at the end for 10 minutes or so.

ROAST PORK WITH TOMATOES, ONIONS AND POTATOES
Roti de porc aux tomates, oignons et pommes de terre

In France pork is roasted without the skin. To those who feel that crackling is the main reason for cooking a pork joint, this will doubtless seem perverse. The skin is prized for other culinary uses - usually to enrich, with its gelatinous qualities as well as its flavour, daubes and other stews, and especially dishes in which the meat is served cold accompanied by the jellied cooking broth. The layer of fat just below the skin is used for barding lean meat to keep it moist during cooking, laid across the top of pâtés and terrines to stop them from getting dry, or layered with potatoes as in the Burgundian crapaudine. The butcher usually removes the bones from the joint and these can be thriftily added to a stock. The French housewife takes home a neatly tied-up joint with just a thin layer of fat on top to keep it moist. Thus the most is extracted from a loin of pork.

Recipes from the French Wine Harvest

FOR 8 PEOPLE
2 kg (aprox 4 lb) joint of loin of pork, (pork roast) boned, and the
rind removed in one piece, not scored as for crackling,
a thin layer of fat remaining on the joint
salt and freshly ground black pepper
500 g (1 lb) ripe tomatoes
250 g (8 oz) onions
1 - 1.5 kg (2 - 3 lb) potatoes

Preheat the oven to gas mark 4, 350°F, 180°C.

Allow 30 minutes per half kilo (1 lb) for a joint weighing up to 2 kg (4 lb), add 20 minutes per half kilo (1 lb) for every half kilo (1 lb) over this weight. Tie the pork up in a neat shape, if the butcher has not already done this, and rub all over with salt and pepper. Put the joint on a rack in the roasting pan and bake in the preheated oven for the appropriate time.

Skin the tomatoes and cut them up roughly. Peel the onions and chop them roughly. Peel the potatoes if you like. If not, just wash them. Large potatoes should be cut up, small ones left whole. An hour before the joint is cooked, add the potatoes to the pan and let them cook in the fat from the joint. About half an hour before serving, add the onions and tomatoes to the pan. If the pork has given off a lot of fat, it is worth at this stage, that is just before adding the onions and tomatoes, spooning some of it off into a bowl to be used at another time to fry potatoes or croûtons.

Slice the joint - easily done since it has been boned - and arrange on a dish with the potatoes, tomatoes, onions and all the cooking juices. This is a no-fail recipe!

ROAST PORK IN PUFF PASTRY WITH GARLIC CLOVES
Roti de Porc en Croute

FOR 8 PEOPLE
2 kg (3 - 4 lb) joint of loin of pork (pork roast)
boned and prepared as above
2 - 3 tablespoons butter
Dijon mustard
500 g (1 lb) puff pastry (frozen can be used)
1 egg
2 - 3 heads of garlic

Preheat the oven to gas mark 6, 400°F, 200°C.

Brown the joint on all sides in the butter. Set aside until it has cooled a little, then spread with Dijon mustard. Roll out the pastry into a rectangle. It must not be too thin or it will burst during the cooking, letting out the juices. Place the joint on top and fold the pastry over quite loosely to make a parcel. Wet the edges with water and press them together. Trim off any extra. This can be used to decorate - cut out leaf shapes or anything else you fancy, wet one side and stick on.

Beat the egg with a little water. Brush over the pastry to give it a nice shiny finish when cooked. Carefully lift the parcel onto a lightly oiled baking sheet. Loosely cover the top of the pastry with foil or greaseproof paper to stop it browning too quickly; you can remove this towards the end of the cooking if you think it is not brown enough. Bake in the preheated oven for about 2 hours, turning down the heat to about gas mark 4, 350°F, 180°C after 30 minutes.

In the meantime, separate the cloves of garlic but do not peel them. Blanch them in boiling water for five minutes. Bake them in the oven round the pork for the final 45 minutes. Make sure everyone who likes garlic gets their fair share to squeeze out of the skins onto their slices of pork. The splendid-looking, golden-brown, pastry parcel can be carved at table.

ROAST GUINEA-FOWL WITH AUTUMN FRUIT
Pintade aux Fruits d'Automne

As guinea-fowl are raised on many of the farms in the Loire they are often on harvest menus.

FOR 4 PEOPLE
approximately 300 ml (½ pint) chicken stock
20 prunes
125 g (4 oz) raisins
4 dessert apples, such as Russets
1 onion
butter
1 guinea-fowl, with liver if possible
125 g (4 oz) sausage-meat
salt and freshly ground black pepper
1 egg, beaten
2 tablespoons redcurrant jelly

Preheat the oven to gas mark 4, 350°F, 180°C.

Heat the stock in a pan and add the prunes and raisins. Simmer for 10 minutes, then strain, keeping the stock on one side.

Chop the onion very finely, or mince it. Brown it in a pan in a little butter. Stone 6 of the prunes, chop them roughly and put them into a bowl with one of the apples, peeled, cored and cut up into small pieces, and half the raisins.

Add the minced liver of the guinea-fowl if available, the sausage-meat and the prepared fruits. Season with salt and pepper. Cook gently for 10 minutes.

Now add a little of the stock to moisten it. Take off the heat and allow to cool slightly before adding the beaten egg to the mixture. Stuff the guinea-fowl with this and sew up the vent.

Heat some more butter in an ovenproof casserole and brown the bird on all sides. When it is browned, season with salt and pepper and add a large glass of the reserved stock. Cover and leave to simmer in the preheated oven for about an hour. The juices are apt to caramelise on the bottom of the pan, so it is best to keep an eye on it and add a little more stock if necessary.

Core and cut the remaining apples in half horizontally. Bake them in their skins, cut side up, in a buttered dish in the oven for about 30 minutes, loosely covered with a piece of buttered foil.

Fifteen minutes before the guinea-fowl is ready, add the remaining prunes and raisins to the casserole.

Serve the guinea-fowl surrounded by the prunes, raisins and baked apples. Melt the redcurrant jelly over a low heat, then spoon over the baked apples.

GUINEA-FOWL WITH BAKED APPLES AND CHESTNUTS
Pintade aux Pommes et Marrons

For pintade aux pommes et marrons, apples are cored and baked in their skins in a buttered tin in the oven. (A variety such as Russets keep their shape. In any case they should be dessert apples, not cookers such as Bramleys.) Chestnuts are peeled, blanched and added to the roasting tin, or substitute vacuum-packed ready-to-use chestnuts, round the guinea-fowl, which is cooked as above.

Rosi Hanson

RUSTIC DUCK STEW WITH SHALLOTS AND POTATOES
Ragoût de Canard

FOR 4 - 6 PEOPLE
1 duck, weighing at least 2.5 kg (5 lb)
butter
a little plain flour
bouquet garni of thyme, parsley,
bay leaf and a stick of celery
12 shallots, peeled
1 kg (2 lb) potatoes
salt and pepper

Joint the duck into manageable pieces, and brown them in butter in a large pan. The duck will give off quite a lot of fat and most of it can be poured off now. (It could be used to fry some potatoes on another occasion, giving them an excellent flavour.)

When the pieces are-well-browned,sprinkle with flour and turn in the butter. Gradually add enough water to cover, stirring and scraping the bottom of the pan to incorporate the flour. Add the bouquet garni and shallots. Bring just to the boil, cover and leave to simmer very gently for about two hours. After one hour add the potatoes, peeled and cut into even sized pieces.

To make a more refined dish, the amount of flour could be reduced or eliminated altogether, and chicken stock used instead of water. In this case, keep the pieces of duck and potatoes warm at the end of the cooking, remove the bouquet garni and boil the stock for about five minutes to reduce it a little and give it a depth of flavour and better consistency.

Check the sauce for seasoning and pour over the duck and potatoes.

CHICKEN COOKED IN WINE WITH ONIONS, MUSHROOMS AND CREAM

Poulet Angevin

The wine used would be local from the area around Angers, such as a Sauvignon de Tourraine or, from slightly further afield, a Muscadet. Rice goes well with this truly delicious dish.

FOR 4 - 6 PEOPLE
1 roasting chicken, weight about 1.5 - 1.75 kg (3 - 3½ lb)
2 tablespoons unsalted butter
12 small onions (as sold for pickling) or shallots, peeled
300 - 500 ml (10 - 15fl oz) dry white wine
250 g (8 oz) button mushrooms
300 ml (10fl oz) thick cream
salt and freshly ground black pepper

Cut up the chicken into 8 pieces i.e. 2 drumsticks, 2 thighs, 2 breasts, but leaving some meat to go with 2 wings (remove wing tips). Melt the butter in a flameproof casserole just big enough to take the pieces of chicken in one layer with the onions fitting in between them. Brown the chicken pieces on all sides in the butter. Once browned, turn down the heat and cook for a further 5 minutes. Add the onions. Cover and cook gently for 15 minutes. Add the wine, which should almost cover the pieces, let it come to the boil, lower the heat, cover and simmer slowly for 15 minutes.

Wipe the mushrooms clean and quarter any large ones. Add to the casserole, basting with the liquid. Simmer for another 10 minutes.

Now remove the chicken, onions and mushrooms with a slotted spoon or skimmer and keep warm in a dish deep enough to allow you to pour the sauce over to serve.

Boil the wine and cooking juices hard to reduce by about half and concentrate the taste. Check frequently, taste after 5 minutes and thereafter until it seems right, remembering that the taste will be diluted by the cream. Add the cream and simmer for a few minutes to heat through. Taste and season. Pour over the chicken and serve.

Rosi Hanson

SAUTÉ OF RABBIT IN A MUSTARD AND CREAM SAUCE
Lapin à la Moutarde

In the simplest version of this family dish, the jointed rabbit is spread with mustard and roasted in the oven for 30 minutes - at the end cream is added to the roasting pan to make the sauce. The method varies from family to family.

FOR 4 PEOPLE
1 large rabbit, jointed
60 g (2 oz) butter
Dijon mustard
1 glass of cognac, about 125 ml (4 fl oz)
salt and freshly ground black pepper
dried thyme
200 g (7 oz) pot of crème fraîche

Preheat the oven to gas mark 3, 325°F, 160°C.

Brown the rabbit joints in the butter in an enamelled cast-iron casserole. This needs to be done over quite a high heat to sear the outside of the meat and seal in the juices, otherwise the rabbit will be dry. When they are browned, smear them quite thickly with Dijon mustard. Warm the cognac in a little pan. Pour it over the rabbit in the casserole and light with a match. When the flames have died down, add salt, pepper and a pinch or two of dried thyme. Bake in the preheated oven, covered, for about 40 minutes.

Remove the casserole from the oven and put it back over a gentle heat on top. Stir the cream into the cooking juices. Let it simmer for five minutes, turning the pieces of rabbit in the sauce. Taste and adjust the seasoning.

Recipes from the French Wine Harvest

ONE POT RABBIT COOKED IN WHITE WINE WITH MUSHROOMS AND POTATOES
Lapin au Sancerre

Recipes similar to this are used in most wine-making areas, using the local wine. Although it cooks for a long time, the preparation time is short; an added advantage is that it is all cooked in one pot, from which it is served.

FOR 6 PEOPLE
250g (8 oz) mushrooms, button or flat as available
1 large rabbit, jointed
1 onion, peeled and thinly sliced
1 tablespoon butter
½ bottle dry white wine
bouquet garni
salt and freshly ground black pepper
12 small potatoes

Prepare the mushrooms by wiping them clean; leave them whole if they are button mushrooms, quarter them if larger.

Brown the pieces of rabbit and the onion in the butter in a flameproof casserole. It is best to sauté the onion first and remove, then turn up the heat for the rabbit. When the rabbit joints have taken colour, deglaze the pan with the white wine, stirring and scraping the bottom of the pan. Now add the bouquet garni, salt, pepper, onions and the mushrooms.

Bring slowly just to the boil. Cover the casserole and let it simmer as gently as possible for 2 hours. This means that it is barely bubbling. It really must not go any faster or will be overcooked and stringy instead of melting and tender.

Wash the potatoes and peel them if you like, but this is not necessary. If you cannot get small potatoes, you will have to use bigger ones and cut them up, but it is not so good as they tend to get mushy round the edges. Twenty or thirty minutes before the rabbit is ready, add them to the casserole to cook on top of the meat.

When they are done, the dish is ready to serve. As you lift the lid of the casserole, a wonderfully appetising smell reminds you how good these simple, rustic, simmered dishes are.

POACHED OX TONGUE WITH MADEIRA SAUCE
Langue de boeuf pot-au-feu, sauce Madère

Tongue, with this traditional sauce, is often served and much appreciated during the harvest. Dry Sercial is the most suitable Madeira to use but, failing that, a Bual or Malmsey, both sweet, could be used, reducing the quantity by half.

FOR 6 - 8 PEOPLE
1 fresh ox tongue, weighing about 2 kg (4 lb)
Poaching vegetables:
1 onion, stuck with two cloves
1 celery stalk
2 carrots
2 small turnips
2 leeks
2 garlic cloves
Bouquet garni of bayleaf and parsley

FOR THE SAUCE:
10 small shallots
250 g (8 oz) smoked streaky bacon in one piece
30 g (1 oz) unsalted butter
15 g (½ oz) plain flour
approximately 600 ml (1 pint) reserved stock
1 teaspoon tomato purée
4 tablespoons dry Madeira (see note above)

The tongue is cooked in exactly the same way as a piece of beef in a pot-au-feu, with the same vegetables - onion stuck with cloves, turnips, carrots, leeks, celery branch, garlic and bouquet garni but omitting the cabbage. Follow the method given in the Burgundy section, but first the tongue must be scrubbed, and soaked in cold water for about two hours. As for the beef, careful skimming is essential, before the vegetables are added.

The tongue will be cooked in 2 to 2½ hours. Drain, reserving the stock, some of which will be needed for the sauce; the remainder can be used in soup. The soggy vegetables should be jettisoned. When the tongue is cool enough to handle, peel off the tough outer skin, which is usually quite easy to do. Cut away any fatty or gristly bits, and the little bones. Now the tongue is ready to be sliced.

To make the sauce, peel the shallots and chop coarsely. Dice the bacon into lardons, little chunks - there is no need to waste time taking off the rind, it is going to be sieved out after giving its flavour.

Melt the butter in a flameproof casserole and brown the shallots and the bacon in it. After about 5 minutes, sprinkle in the flour and stir. Add a little of the stock. Stir well, scraping the little bits off the bottom of the pan. As it thickens, add the rest of the stock, then the tomato purée. Bring to the boil, turn down the heat, cover and simmer very gently for 30 to 45 minutes.

Just before serving, sieve the sauce, then add the Madeira. Put the sliced tongue into the casserole with the sauce, making sure it covers it, and simmer until it is warmed through.

Any extra sauce can be handed round in a sauce-boat. Serve with rice. (A brined tongue could be used, but will need soaking in fresh water for about 24 hrs, changing the water regularly).

Rosi Hanson

MME COTAT'S CARAMELISED RHUBARB CAKE
Gâteau de Rhubarbe

This cake is equally good made with sliced apples, pears, apricots, pineapple, blackberries or cherries.

FOR 6 PEOPLE
110 gr plain flour
60 gr caster sugar
3 tablespoons milk
2 tablespoons cooking oil (a light olive or sunflower oil is suitable)
1 egg
1 teaspoon baking powder
750g - 1 kg (1½ - 2 lb) rhubarb, trimmed and cut into short equal lengths

FOR THE CARAMEL SAUCE:
125 g (4 oz) sugar
90 g (3 oz) butter
1 egg

Preheat the oven to gas mark 8, 450°F, 230°C.

Mix all the ingredients, except the fruit, together in a bowl to make quite a soft, almost runny, dough. Butter a 23 cm (9 in) round sponge tin. Sprinkle with flour. Spread the mixture into it. Place the rhubarb pieces on top of the mixture.

It is a little difficult to be accurate about the amount of rhubarb which can give off a lot of liquid – but bear in mind it is a very soft cake. The sharpness of the rhubarb will be offset by the caramel.

Bake in the preheated oven for about 30 minutes, until golden. (It will rise a little.)

Meanwhile, prepare the caramel sauce. Melt the sugar and butter together in a small pan. Remove from the heat, cool a little, then stir in the egg. When you take the cake out of the oven, pour this sauce over it. Put it under a hot grill for two minutes or until the sauce has caramelised. Watch it carefully, as it burns easily. Leave the cake to cool. It may be eaten warm or cold.

WHITE WINE CAKE
Gâteau au Vin Blanc

This simply-made cake is light and delicious, much nicer than it sounds! It is good with compôtes, poached fruit of any kind, vanilla custard, or sliced and spread with jam or chocolate.

FOR 4 PEOPLE
3 eggs
250 g (8 oz) caster sugar
1 pinch of salt
grated zest of 1 lemon
75 ml (2½ fl oz) sunflower or groundnut oil
100 ml (3½ fl oz) white wine
175 g (6 oz) plain flour
1 teaspoon baking powder
butter for greasing

Preheat the oven to gas mark 5, 375°F, 190°C.

Butter a 23 cm (9 in) sponge tin or small charlotte mould.

Beat the eggs, sugar, salt and lemon zest together until white. Add the oil and wine and continue beating for two more minutes. Sift the flour and baking powder together and incorporate into the mixture.

Pour into the tin and bake in the preheated oven for about 40 minutes. Turn out of the mould onto a cooling rack.

Rosi Hanson

MARINATED PEARS IN PUFF PASTRY PIE
Tarte aux Poires

FOR 6 - 8 PEOPLE
750 g (1½ lb) ripe dessert pears

FOR THE MARINADE:
60 g (2 oz) caster sugar
a little freshly ground black pepper
4 tablespoons cognac

FOR THE TART:
500 g (1 lb) frozen puff pastry, ready to use
1 egg
a little extra caster sugar

Peel and core the pears. Slice finely and put into a bowl. Sprinkle with the sugar and cognac. Grind a little black pepper over them. Turn them in this mixture from time to time and leave to marinate for 2 to 3 hours. Roll out the pastry. Butter a 24 cm (9½ in) tart tin. Line it with the pastry, keeping aside enough to make the lid later. Chill the pastry-lined tart tin in the fridge for 30 to 60 minutes.

Put a heavy baking sheet in the oven and preheat to gas mark 7, 425°F, 220°C.

Lift the pears out of the marinade with a skimmer and arrange on the pastry base. Keep the marinading liquid to use when the tart is baked. Use the remaining pastry to make a lid. Wet the edges with water and press together to seal. Use any trimmings to cut shapes and decorate the lid, sticking them on with a little water. Prick the lid with a fork several times.

Break the egg into a bowl and beat lightly. Brush this over the lid. Shake some sugar over it and bake in the preheated oven on the baking sheet for 20 minutes.

The marinade can be served in a jug, and/or with a bowl of thick crème fraîche.

Recipes from the French Wine Harvest

VERY FAST SALAD OF GRAPES AND APPLES IN SWEET WHITE WINE
Salade Vigneronne

The grapes used for this are sweet table grapes, although traditionally it would be Chasselas which used to be widely planted round Pouilly-sur-Loire, making white wine for everyday consumption. Now they have largely been replaced by Sauvignon Blanc and the Chasselas is grown as a table grape further south.

FOR 4 PEOPLE
150 g (5 oz) white table grapes
150 g (5 oz) black table grapes
2 crisp eating apples
50 g (2 oz) caster (superfine) sugar
250 ml (8 fl oz) sweet white wine (vin doux)
such as Coteaux du Layon, (or it could be a Sauternes or Barsac)

Wash the grapes and pat them dry, take them off the stalk. If there are pips and you have time, take them out.

Peel, if you wish, and core the apples. Slice them finely.

Put the grapes and apples in a shallow bowl, sprinkle with sugar and shake the bowl to mix the fruit and sugar together. Pour over the wine and keep in the fridge till ready to serve.

CHAMPAGNE

Synonymous with celebration, champagne is the world's favourite party wine - that is, for those who can afford it. But until approximately the middle of the nineteenth century the textile trade was as important as wine to Rheims, the great cathedral city which is the commercial centre of the champagne trade. It was in the eighteenth century that sparkling champagne became popular at the court of the Regent, Philippe Duc d'Orléans; then later, Mme de Pompadour, who is supposed to have held that champagne is 'the only wine that leaves a woman beautiful after drinking it,' gave it the seal of her approval. It has been drunk by the rich and famous ever since.

Unlike most other wine-growing areas of France, in Champagne few growers vinify and bottle their own produce, perhaps because of the great expense involved in the special process known as the méthode champenoise (champagne method). It is estimated that about half the grapes grown in the Champagne region are sold by the growers to big merchants, firms with a world-wide reputation, such as Bollinger, Krug, Moët and Chandon, Mumm, Veuve Clicquot and Louis Roederer, who vinify them. The balance is vinified by large co-operative groupings of growers or individual growers, who mainly sell their champagne to French private customers although "Growers' Champagne" has become a fashionable niche market further afield in recent years.

Three main grapes are planted: Chardonnay and Pinot Noir (as in Burgundy) and the Pinot Meunier. It is a curious fact that champagne, which is mainly white (though sometimes pink) is made from two red grapes (the Pinot Noir and Pinot Meunier). The grapes are pressed almost immediately after they have been picked and the red colouring matter in the skins does not come into contact with the juice (unless a rose´ champagne is being made when there will be brief contact).

Over the centuries Champagne has been the scene of many bloody battles. Now it seems rather peaceful, with fertile hectares given over to wheat-growing on a grand scale. Cemeteries and memorials to British, American and Commonwealth soldiers are a poignant reminder, however, of the area's tragic past during two Battles of the Marne in the First World War.

The vineyards are on rolling chalk hillsides (the same band of chalk which makes the cliffs of Dover so famously white) from which have been carved hundreds of kilometres of cool underground cellars. These are crucial to the making of fine champagne, which undergoes a second fermentation in bottle during the spring following the autumn in which the grapes were picked and vinified. The carbon dioxide produced in this fermentation (which requires sustained cool temperatures) dissolves into the wine, giving the characteristic sparkle.

The Champenois have developed a method over many decades for removing the spent yeasts which have brought about this sparkle - they freeze the neck of the bottle which is held upside-down in a brine bath, having previously shaken the yeast deposit down onto the cork (a process known as remuage, translated as riddling); the deposit is trapped in the frozen bullet of champagne, so when the closure is removed, it is shot out by the pressure inside the bottle (dégorgement or disgorging). The bottle must then be topped up and a proper champagne cork and its wire muzzle put on. It is easy to see that this process is a skilful, labour-intensive one, although it is now mostly mechanised.

Champagne is not normally sold with the name of its village or vineyard of origin on the label. Instead, the big Champagne merchant houses buy or grow their own grapes in many different communes and create their own blends. The region is divided into three districts: the Montagne de Reims, the Vallée de la Marne and the Côte des Blancs. Tradition has it that Dom Pérignon, a seventeenth century monk at the Abbey of Hautvillers on a hillside above Epernay (now one of the centres for champagne-making) first tasted and blended grapes from different villages to produce a perfectly balanced champagne. He is also credited with the first use of corks, which, after all, make sparkling champagne as we know it today, possible.

Rosi Hanson

CHAMPAGNE AND CABBAGE

In her kitchen in Le Mesnil sur Oger - vineyards can be seen from the window - Mme Bernadette Emprin is making boulettes for her grandsons' lunch and talking about the harvests of her youth. Boulettes have not changed - delicious little 'bullets' of highly seasoned, minced meat - but the harvest has.

In her youth, she says, all the pickers were lodged and fed. It was essential; now it is becoming rare. The pickers left on foot for the vines early in the morning after a quick coffee. Everyone was given a panier (a basket to put the grapes in), a pair of secateurs and a goblet, attached to their belt when not in use, for the duration of the harvest - woe betide any harvester foolish and careless enough to lose any of their equipment - they would have to pay for it. At about 8.45 the chef d'équipe distributed a breakfast, which was eaten standing round a little fire of dry vine shoots, and consisted of bread, a piece of salami, liver pâté, brawn and maybe a piece of the local cheese, Maroilles (the traditional harvest cheese). They were soon back at work.

The sight of the horse and cart arriving just after midday must have been welcome, for work went on whatever the weather. Lunch, unloaded from the cart, was eaten in the vines. One tin plate each served for soup and a slice of meat and a vegetable. If you wanted fruit, you picked a handful of grapes.

The evening meal hardly varied - one day soupe aux choux, one day pot-au-feu: good dishes in themselves but monotonous day in, day out.

So those were the good old days … and the impression Mme Emprin gives is that you can keep them. Nostalgia is for those who did not have to do the work. But Mme Emprin, a redoubtable lady and admired cook, was happy to go on helping in the harvest kitchen of a nearby vigneron cousin, a member of the co-operative Union Champagne.

Recipes from the French Wine Harvest

Soupe aux choux, otherwise known as potée champenoise, and pot-au-feu are traditional favourites. The potée positively bulges with a variety of vegetables and different cuts of salted pork and very often a large smoked sausage. In the pot-au-feu, the traditional assembly of meats is often augmented by a fine ox tongue, which gives the cook a chance to use the beef for boulettes or hachis Parmentier and to serve the tongue, sliced, with a Madeira sauce, fresh tomato sauce or a vinaigrette.

There is, naturally, always a vegetable soup in the evening to start things off. 'Toujours une soupe le soir' is the unchanging refrain to the harvest songs which are the menus throughout French vineyard areas. Rare is the harvest household which has given up this particular tradition. Nobody seems to follow a recipe. One thing is certain, harvesters in Champagne, who are usually from the north of France, eat a lot of soup - three helpings can disappear in a trice.

In the evening, soup might be followed by potato omelettes, then a green salad, cheese and maybe a traditional wine-maker's tarte aux raisins (grape tart) if it is an abundant crop but certainly not if it is a year in which the vines have suffered frost and only produced a small crop.

Another evening there might be a salade au lard, a salad of dandelion leaves with hot bacon. The salad used to be made from the tender young leaves of dandelions growing between the rows of vines. Now, most vines receive so many treatments (against mildew, oidium, grey rot, etc.) that the leaves must be grown in the kitchen garden or bought from the local market. It remains a wonderful dish, with the slight bitterness of the leaves counteracted by the bacon and by a little red wine vinegar mixed with the melted fat given off in the frying, which makes the dressing for the salad. Curly endive can make a good alternative. Another favourite country salad consists of potatoes (small long ones) sautéed with little bits of streaky bacon and onions, mixed with an escarole lettuce with a sharpish dressing and served while still warm. These salads can make an excellent, simple lunch, with a piece of cheese and fruit to follow.

Rosi Hanson

AN INDEPENDENT CHAMPAGNE GROWER'S HARVEST

Larmandier Père et Fils in the village of Vertus is one of the independent growers in Champagne who make and bottle their own wine and sell it themselves under their own label. The family owns about 9 hectares (22 acres) in Cramant and the champagne they make from this is particularly respected. They make several other Grand Cru and Premier Cru champagnes, as well as a small quantity of red wine - Côteaux Champenois-Vertus Rouge - something of a rarity. They export increasingly, but most of their wine is sold to private customers who like, as so many French wine-lovers do, to drive to the vineyards, taste in the cellars, make their choice and give their order directly to the person who made it, taking their case or two away with them.

It is the custom of the Larmandiers to assemble all their pickers the night before the harvest starts and to drink a glass (une flute - the tall champagne glass which shows off to perfection the beautiful sight of the rising bubbles) of their champagne together before sitting down to dinner. They are usually 35 to 40 at table, with about 24 being lodged.

The day starts with breakfast of coffee, tea or hot chocolate, bread, butter and jam, but a more serious breakfast is consumed in the vines at about nine o'clock, when there is a half-hour break for charcuterie and cheese and bread, which Mme Larmandier takes up to the vines herself. If the day is cold, there are hot drinks served around a brazier.

Game, such as wild boar and pheasant, are sometimes on the menu here, for M. Larmandier enjoys shooting. Poulet au champagne, lapin au champagne (chicken and rabbit respectively, cooked in champagne) and potée champenoise are among the local dishes. Blanquettes, roast pork, lentils with meaty little sausages, boudins blancs (white sausages made from a smooth-textured mixture of chicken or rabbit and pork, with cream, eggs and onions), chicory wrapped in ham with a cheese sauce, are some of the other lovely French family dishes which are to be found here. Desserts include the ever-popular standby, egg custards, clafoutis and tarte vite-fait aux pommes (quickly-made apple tart). At least once every two days, says Mme Larmandier with some pride, the pickers have a bottle of champagne with their meal. On Sundays at mid-day, the Larmandiers offer their pickers an aperitif of ratafia, a drink made like wine until the fermentation of sugars in the grape juice is stopped by the addition of marc or brandy. It is these little traditions, these extra attentions, different in each family, which create the atmosphere for which many pickers return year after year.

For many French people a festive meal must finish with a bottle of sparkling wine, champagne if possible, drunk with the dessert and/or little biscuits or brioche. For the end of harvest celebration dinner, known locally as le cochelet (most areas have their own expression), Mme Larmandier chooses a more elegant first course than usual, followed by leg of lamb and the dessert is usually ice cream flavoured with marc de champagne (local brandy) in the shape of champagne bottles, accompanied, naturally, by their own champagne.

FEEDING THE 600 PICKERS AT LOUIS ROEDERER

Among the great champagne houses - many of whom are part of multi-national concerns - Roederer is one of the largest land-owners. It has remained a private, family-owned company and this certainly creates a different feeling. Cristal Roederer is a blend that was created for Tsar Alexander II in 1876 and its clear crystal bottle is still the epitome of elegance.

There are seven vineyard properties in the best villages, comprising 450 well-situated acres growing 75% of the grapes needed to make the 2.5 million bottles sold each year. During the harvest 600 pickers are fed and housed. The scale of the exercise is mind-boggling.

That the whole thing runs like clockwork is due to the efficiency of the ladies who are in charge of each of the seven harvest kitchens. Provisions are ordered centrally and delivered daily, with each of the cooks phoning in her requirements.

In the high-ceilinged old dining-room at Ay the wood-burning stove is lit and 90 pickers are sitting down to dinner. They badly need a hot meal. The weather conditions have been atrocious. The brightly coloured oilskins provided by the company have been in use all day; as showers drenched the vineyards. Lunch, boeuf mode (beef slow cooked in wine with carrots) sent up to the vineyards in huge metal containers called norvégiennes, was eaten in the muddy fields under gloomy, grey skies.

In the kitchen they know a morale-raiser is needed. They are sending out tureens of clear soup with vermicelli, to be followed by a rice salad with tomatoes, gherkins, olives, hard-boiled eggs and tuna fish. Potée champenoise comes next - the large, steaming plates of salt pork, smoked sausages and colourful piles of vegetables are bound to raise the spirits. By the time the locally-made Brie cheese is passed round everyone is feeling much better and the tarte aux prunes (open-faced plum tart) completes the transformation.

In the kitchen they are waiting for word that the vat-house workers are ready to eat. They are rarely able to leave the fermenting grapes at normal mealtimes and send a member of the team across the yard to warn the kitchen that they will be ready in fifteen minutes. Their work is crucial, they work long hours and the cooks are sympathetic, ready to spoil them with their favourite dishes and with plenty of cakes to keep them going when they are working late.

FIVE VEGETABLE SOUP
Potage aux Cinq Légumes

Many and various are the vegetable soups made by harvest cooks, depending on what ingredients are in the garden or market. 'Bonne femme' (mainly onions, leeks and potatoes) and 'potage Crécy' (mainly carrots) are two old favourites among the thick soups. These creamy-textured soups do not need a stock base. In general, the peeled vegetables are chopped and sweated in butter, water is added, brought to the simmer and when the vegetables are soft but not sodden, the whole is put through a mouli-légumes or liquidised. This unusual combination of vegetables gives an excellent, very fresh-tasting soup.

FOR 6 PEOPLE
4 medium carrots
3 medium potatoes
2 medium turnips (the French purple and white variety)
1 round lettuce
3 leeks 30 - 45 g (1 - 1½ oz) butter
1 litre (1¾ pints) water
salt and freshly ground black pepper

Peel the root vegetables and wash the lettuce. Wash and trim the leeks. Chop everything roughly. Melt the butter in a pan, add the vegetables, cover and sweat for about 10 minutes. Add the water, bring to a simmer and leave to cook gently for 20 to 30 minutes. It is important not to overcook the vegetables. Put through the medium blade of a mouli-légumes or liquidise: the soup should not have too fine a texture. Taste and add seasoning. Heat through and serve, sprinkled with chopped parsley, and maybe a spoonful of cream stirred in at the last minute.

POTÉE CHAMPENOISE

Potée, a sort of cross between a soup and stew, is rustic, comforting food. Colloquially it is sometimes called soupe aux choux. Many regions have their own version (some areas call it a garbure). Cabbage and salt pork are usually the main ingredients. It is hard to give exact quantities - what follows is a guide - as everyone has his or her own preference about which vegetables, and how much of them, to include.

Petit salé, sold in most charcuteries in France, is used in a number of rustic dishes and has an excellent flavour. It is a way of salting various different cuts of pork in order to preserve them; a dry salt cure is used, consisting of salt, saltpetre, sugar, spices and herbs. In this recipe the leaner end of the belly of pork is used, or a mixture of cuts if preferred, particularly if you are making it in a larger quantity. Use green streaky bacon in a piece or salted belly of pork

FOR 6 - 8 PEOPLE
500 g (1 lb) salt pork ('petit salé' - see introduction)
250 g (8 oz) dried haricot beans
2-3 leeks
12 small or 6 medium-sized carrots
6 small turnips
2 medium-sized onions

bouquet garni made of 1 stick of celery,
2 bay leaves, a few sprigs of thyme (fresh or dry)
and parsley
1 large smoked pork boiling sausage, if liked
6 medium-sized potatoes, peeled
1 savoy cabbage
pepper

The first step, the night before, is to soak the joint of salted pork. Change the water several times. The dried beans also need to be soaked in water overnight.

Cover the pork with fresh cold water and bring slowly to the boil in a pan. Use a skimmer to remove the scum which rises as it comes to the boil. As in the method for pot-au-feu, this is an important step from the point of view of the clarity of the stock. Simmer for about 30 minutes.

Meanwhile, peel and roughly chop the leeks, carrots, turnips and onions into quite large pieces. Prepare a bouquet garni. Add the vegetables and herbs to the pork after the first 30 minutes, bring back to the boil and continue to simmer for another 30 to 45 minutes.

Drain the haricot beans and bring them to the boil in fresh water. Cover and simmer until nearly done - about 45 minutes, but best to test for yourself. Drain them and finish their cooking in some of the meat and vegetable stock. You are going to need some for cooking the potatoes also, so ladle out enough for both vegetables.

Boil the sausage in water for about 45 minutes.

Cut the potatoes into even sizes and cook in the stock.

Quarter and core the cabbage and boil in water separately.

It sounds as if a miracle of organisation must be achieved, but in fact, exact timings are not very important. In many households all the ingredients are added, at intervals, to the same pot, thus saving a lot of washing-up. Unfortunately, the cabbage (and the smoked sausage if included) tend to overwhelm the other flavours and the stock is more or less unusable for soup for another meal. It is hard to judge the cooking time of the potatoes and haricot beans if they are included in the general melée of vegetables in a large pot and although it does not really matter if they disintegrate, you end up with a mushy purée which thickens the stock. It may sound rather a fiddle to have different ingredients cooking in separate pots (and the washer-up may complain), but it is nicer.

Assemble all the vegetables and meats, with one or two ladles of the stock, in one splendid, steaming dish. Put a pot of Dijon mustard on the table.

Recipes from the French Wine Harvest

CABBAGE AND BACON TO SERVE WITH PORK CHOPS OR SAUSAGES
Potées Choux

A cabbage dish, but rather confusingly, not the same thing as potée champenoise. At Roederer's they fill an enormous cauldron with cabbages when they make this vegetable dish for their pickers.

FOR 6 - 8 PEOPLE
1 medium Savoy cabbage
250 g (8 oz) smoked streaky bacon in one piece

Start by boiling the cabbage, quartered and cored, in water. While it is boiling for 5 to 10 minutes you have time to remove the rind from the bacon and chop it into dice. Drain the cabbage well and chop it finely. Put a flameproof casserole over a moderate heat on top of the stove. Add the bacon and let the fat melt. Add the cabbage and mix it with the bacon. Stir for a few minutes over the heat so that the cabbage finishes cooking. Serve it with potatoes and pork chops, or with grilled sausages.

SALAD OF GREEN LEAVES AND POTATOES WITH HOT BACON
Salade au Lard

FOR 6 PEOPLE
1 bunch dandelion leaves or
1 head escarole or frisée lettuce
250g (8 oz) green streaky bacon in a piece
red wine vinegar
black pepper

Wash and dry the salad leaves, then place them in a serving bowl. Remove the rind from the bacon and dice. Let your frying pan get hot, then throw in the bacon - it sizzles and the fat melts. When crisp add to the salad.
Now quickly deglaze the frying pan with a little red wine vinegar and pour the 'dressing' - vinegar and bacon fat - over the salad, grind some pepper over it and eat while warm. Sad to say, a lot of bacon now gives off water rather than fat, in which case you are better off throwing this away and warming a little olive oil in the pan before deglazing with the vinegar.

SALAD OF HOT POTATOES, LEAVES, BACON AND ONIONS
Salade de Pommes de Terre Chaudes, du Lard et des Oignons

For this dish you need to use waxy potatoes - varieties such as Fir Apple Pinks, Charlotte, Kipfler or Roseval.

FOR 6 - 8 PEOPLE
500g (1 lb) potatoes
250(8 oz) smoked or green streaky bacon in a piece
1 medium onion, or several shallots
1 head of escarole or frisée lettuce
oil and vinegar
black pepper

Wash but do not peel the potatoes. Cut each into about four, depending on size. Dice the bacon, having removed the rind. Peel and chop the onion or shallots. Wash and dry the salad leaves, then place them in a serving bowl large enough to allow you to turn all the ingredients vigorously. Heat a pan over a moderate heat and put in the bacon. Let the fat melt, then sauté the potatoes and onion in it. Keep stirring and scraping the bottom of the pan, so that everything becomes crispy without burning. If you feel the bacon has not given off enough fat, add some oil. Eat as soon as you mix the contents of the pan with the escarole dressed lightly with oil, vinegar and black pepper, ready in the serving bowl.

RICE SALAD WITH TUNA
Salade de Riz au Thon

FOR 6 - 8 PEOPLE
375 g (12 oz) white long-grain rice
olive oil and wine vinegar for vinaigrette
salt and freshly ground black pepper
3 hard-boiled eggs
500 g (1 lb) tomatoes
a few small gherkins
125 g (4 oz) green or black olives
1 medium sized tin of tuna, preferably in olive oil

Boil the rice as directed on the packet, or using your normal method, and taking care not to overcook. Drain thoroughly and mix immediately with a vinaigrette in a serving bowl. Season well with salt and pepper and leave to cool. This can be done ahead of time.

Shortly before the meal, shell the eggs and core the tomatoes. Slice the eggs, tomatoes and gherkins. Break up the tuna into chunks. Carefully fold all the ingredients, including the olives, into the rice salad and serve.

RABBIT COOKED IN CHAMPAGNE
Lapin au Champagne

No-one is going to buy a bottle of champagne just in order to use a glass in a rabbit stew. But if you plan to have a bottle of champagne, you could consider appropriating a glass for the kitchen - it makes a wonderful dish! Or you could substitute a glass of dry white wine. Similarly, if rabbit is hard to come by, this recipe works well for chicken.

FOR 6 PEOPLE
1 large rabbit, jointed
1 tablespoon butter
12 small onions or 1 medium onion
1 tablespoon plain flour
1 glass of champagne
thyme
bay leaf
salt and freshly ground black pepper

Place the butter in a flameproof casserole over a medium heat and brown the pieces of rabbit in it well.

Add the peeled onions (if you cannot get small pickling-type onions, use a finely sliced, medium onion). Sprinkle with flour, turning the pieces of rabbit so they are well coated and the flour browns.

Add a glass of champagne, stirring as it bubbles, in order to deglaze the pan. As the flour and wine thicken, add enough water to barely cover the meat. Add a pinch of dried thyme, or several sprigs if it is fresh, and a bay leaf, salt and pepper. Cover and simmer slowly for about an hour until tender. Serve with steamed potatoes or rice.

PARCELS OF VEAL ESCALOPES FILLED WITH PORK AND HERBS
Paupiettes de Veau

FOR 6 PEOPLE
250 g (8 oz) minced pork
salt and freshly ground black pepper
6 thin veal escalopes
enough pork back-fat, or streaky bacon to wrap up each of the parcels of veal and pork
2 cloves of garlic
parsley
15 - 30g (½ - 1 oz) butter
approximately 150 ml (5fl oz) water
bouquet garni (parsley, thyme and bay)

Season the pork well, adding chopped garlic and plenty of chopped parsley. Lay each escalope flat. Put a spoonful of the pork mixture on each and roll up, tucking in the ends. Wrap each one in a piece of the fat to keep it moist during cooking and tie it up like a parcel with string.

Brown the parcels very well in the butter in a casserole into which they just fit. Pour away the excess fat before adding water and deglazing. It is easier to do this if you remove the veal to a plate, then replace it. Add the bouquet garni. Bring back just to the boil, cover and simmer very gently - too fast and the meat will toughen - for an hour or slightly longer.

BEEF BRAISED IN RED WINE WITH CARROTS
Boeuf mode/ Boeuf Braisé

This traditional dish, ideal for feeding a large party, turns up in every wine region and in a good many other places too. The basic principle is that you take a cheap piece of beef and cook it very slowly with onions and carrots in wine, flavoured with herbs. It differs from a daube in that the beef is cooked in one piece, not cut up. It is more correctly called boeuf à la mode. It is sometimes known as boeuf à la cuillère, because it should be tender enough to cut with a spoon rather than a knife.

There are many recipes: Julia Child is definitive in her 'Mastering the Art of French Cooking' Vol.1 and in 'French Provincial Cooking' Elizabeth David is very good on the cold version, in which calves' feet are cooked with the meat, giving natural gelatine to the stock. When cold, the meal is sliced and surrounded by carrots. The stock is allowed to cool so that the fat may be easily removed. It is clarified if necessary. It is then poured over the meal and carrots and sets to a rich jelly. It makes a wonderful sight - the dark jelly with the meat and orange carrots just visible beneath it - and wonderful eating – great for a buffet party. Like pot-au-feu, there are no strict rules. Harvest kitchens are busy places and the cooks are likely to simplify. A version with more depth of flavour calls for the beef to be marinated in wine and herbs overnight. It uses stock as well as wine in the cooking.

During its cooking the meat will shrink, a point to bear in mind when calculating how much you need. It is certainly much better to cook a piece that is too big. Small pieces just do not lend themselves to long slow cooking. Left-overs can be used in several delicious ways, e.g. stuffed tomatoes, stuffed peppers, hachis Parmentiers, boulettes, or reheated as a miroton (see below). Extra stock can be turned into a consommé and served with rice or vermicelli cooked in it, or with diced fresh vegetables (a mixture of carrots, turnips, celery, tomatoes, for example) lightly poached in it, with some fresh herbs added at the end (coriander can be a spectacular success, parsley is fine). These ideas are just jumping-off points, the sort of thing a French housewife might do.

If you would like to cook this for a party, you might like to know that for 40 people you would need 7.5 kg (15 lb) meat, 4 pigs' trotters and 3 bottles of wine.

FOR A HOT BOEUF MODE FOR ABOUT 10 PEOPLE

approximately 2 - 2½ kg (4 - 5 lb) joint of beef:
rump, topside or silverside are appropriate, boned and,
if necessary, tied up to make a neat shape
3 tablespoons pork fat or cooking oil
water or beef or veal stock
2 pig's trotters split in two, or 1 calf's foot split,
to give body to the stock, if liked. If neither are available,
you could use a large piece of fresh pork rind
15 g (½ oz) cornflour or arrowroot, optional
1 tablespoon Madeira or port, optional
1 - 1½ kg (2 - 3 lb) carrots
30 small onions, often called pickling onions,
if available

FOR THE MARINADE:

2 carrots, 2 onions, 2 celery stalks, 2 cloves garlic,
all peeled and roughly chopped
bouquet garni of parsley, bay leaf and thyme
6 allspice berries
6 peppercorns
salt
1 bottle of red wine, neither too acid nor too tannic as these elements become
concentrated in the cooking, perhaps a Gamay from the Loire or Beaujolais

Place the beef in a large bowl with the marinade ingredients. Turn the meat from time to time, when you remember, and leave about 12 hours (overnight is usually most convenient, but you are not expected to rise from your bed to turn the meat).

If you wish to skip this step, assemble all these marinade ingredients ready to use in the cooking. Drain and dry the meat. Heat the fat or oil in a large flameproof casserole and brown the piece of meat well on all sides. Pour in a little of the marinade and deglaze the pan, scraping the bottom with a wooden spoon. Add the rest of the wine and the vegetables, herbs and spices. Make up the liquid with water or stock so that it reaches about two thirds of the way up the beef. Add the calf's foot or the trotters. Bring just to the boil. Cover and simmer very gently and steadily for about 3½ hours.

In the meantime peel and prepare the carrots and little onions. Cook them separately in a little of the stock taken from the pot. If you were to cook them in with the beef you would get a rather sweet and very carroty tasting stock for the sauce or next day's soup. Also, it is nicer to have these vegetables slightly crunchy and not soggy as they would be if cooked slowly with the beef.

When the beef is cooked, lift it out and keep it warm while you deal with the sauce. Taste the stock and decide what it needs. Strain and return to the pan. Do you want to put some aside as it is to make a soup? Do you want to reduce it, by fast boiling? Or do you want to thicken it with a little cornflour mixed with Madeira or port, as suggested by Julia Child? If so, beat in this mixture and simmer for 3 minutes. Does it need more seasoning?

Add the ready-cooked carrots and onions and simmer for a few minutes, while you slice the beef. Arrange the meat and vegetables on a dish, pour over the sauce and serve.

BEEF MIROTON

This is a way of using up beef from a pot-au-feu and it works well for left-over boeuf mode if you have both beef and stock. For half a kilo (1 lb) of sliced beef, take half a kilo (1 lb) of onions. Peel and slice the onions finely. Cook them very gently in 30 g (1 oz) of butter - do not let them brown - they should be soft and yellow. Add a scant tablespoon of flour and stir it in. Start adding some beef stock, stirring as you go, to make a sauce. You will probably need about 300 ml (½ pint) of stock. Lay the slices of beef in the sauce, put a lid on the pan and heat it through.

QUICK TART OF APPLES OR PEARS
Tarte Suisse/Tarte Vite-Fait

FOR 6 PEOPLE
1 egg
3 tablespoons milk
2 tablespoons oil
(such as groundnut or sunflower)
5 tablespoons plain flour
3 tablespoons fine semolina
(you can find this in Italian stores)
1 pinch salt
1 teaspoon baking powder
2 tablespoons kirsch or other
fruit brandy, if liked

FOR THE FILLING:
500 g (1 lb) dessert apples or ripe pears
icing sugar for sprinkling

Preheat the oven to gas mark 6-7, 400-450°F, 200-250°C. Put a heavy baking sheet in the middle. Butter a 23 cm (9 inch) tart tin.

Peel, core and thinly slice the apples or pears. Put all the other ingredients into a mixer and blend, or beat all the ingredients with a whisk till amalgamated. Pour the mixture, which is quite a liquid dough, into the greased tart tin.

Spread the sliced fruit over the mixture in the tin - there should be plenty of fruit. Add sugar if you feel the fruit needs it. Sprinkle apples with cinnamon if you wish.

Bake on top of the baking sheet in the preheated oven for 15 to 20 minutes. Mme Larmandier says it is quite gooey, although if you forget it and cook it too long, it is still good. Just before serving, sprinkle with icing sugar - it can be eaten warm or cold and is good with cream or vanilla ice cream.

ALSACE

Alsace is a good example of the importance of geographical location to wine. The influence of the Vosges mountains is paramount. Alsace is very far north in wine-making terms and without the favourable protection of the Vosges, these vineyards would not exist. The vines are planted on the east side, where they catch the rising sun. The soil is relatively dry, as the rain coming in from the Atlantic falls on the west side of the mountain range. Vines do not need a lot of moisture, in fact quite the reverse, as the grapes suffer from rot if they get too wet.

Early on a Sunday morning in autumn the market around the church of St Joseph in the city of Colmar is being set up. Stallholders are arranging mounds of dark red beetroot with their vivid green leaves and varieties of large, long radishes: black, red and snowy white; pale green stacks of kohlrabi contrast with little cream turnips, tinged with pink. Cardoons with their beautiful grey-green foliage take up a lot of room on one or two stalls. On another, a stall holder cuts a slice of pumpkin and displays it to show off the bright orange flesh. There are still-life arrangements here to rival the riches of Colmar's museum. One woman has brought wild mushrooms gathered in the forests and at the neighbouring stall her friend has some local farmhouse Munster cheese, which is very pale orange, quite unlike the commercial variety. A man at another stall has only a loaf of bread for sale, but it is 2.25 metres (7½ feet) long, weighs 23 kilos (over 40 lb) and it has been baked for four hours in a wood-fired oven. It has a blackened crust and cream-coloured crumb and is made from a mixture of wheat, barley and oat flour. People are soon lining up to buy a slice.

Recipes from the French Wine Harvest

Leaving the city, the route des vins takes you through pretty countryside with lovely stands of trees among the vineyards and a succession of villages each more picturesque than the last. Two of the most famous of these, Riquewihr and Ribeauvillé, are much visited - the proximity of the border makes it a favourite with Germans - and the prevalence of souvenir shops all selling the same decorated Alsace pottery is a little tiresome. However, the charm of the ancient, narrow streets - in Eguisheim, for instance - and the almost dazzling displays of geraniums falling from every balcony, are extremely beguiling. Above all, the villages are neat and tidy - the only exception being the big bundles of sticks, haphazardly arranged and precariously balanced on top of church spires and the towers of municipal buildings; these curious constructions are storks' nests.

It is not like any other part of France. Many people here speak Alsace's own language at home and French in public; local people are apt to refer to the rest of France as l'Intérieure, the Interior.

Delightful wrought-iron signs hang outside many shops and businesses illustrating their wares, often humorously. Pâtisseries sell kugelhopf and other local cakes. You can buy and eat the local savoury tart, tarte flambée, straight from the oven at mid-day and evening. The pastry is rolled out as thinly as possible and it is baked at high heat in a baker's oven before the bread goes in. The dishes here make use of many of the typical northern European ingredients - but with a French touch - notably in choucroute garni and other pork dishes, and there are plenty of quite reasonably-priced places to eat them, together with a glass or two of local beer or wine.

Because it is so far north, little red wine is made here: a small amount of Pinot Noir is cultivated. But Alsace is famous for the aromatic, white grape types, which thrive in this climate, each of them giving very different styles of wine. Traditionally the wines are known by the names of the grapes, rather than by village or vineyard names. However, now the finest vineyards have been identified and classified as Grands Crus and we find the precise names of origin appearing more frequently on Alsace wine labels.

Riesling is intensely fruity, with lively acidity, and ages well. Gewürztraminer is spicy (gewürz means spicy in German) and is often round and soft to taste. It should not really have any residual sugar but it feels sweet on the palate because of its ripeness and low acidity. Pinot Gris gives a full-bodied wine, sometimes described as slightly smoky in flavour. Like Gewürztraminer, the wine can be round, rich, ripe and low in acidity but not actually sweet. These are the grape types believed by the Alsace growers to be the best and are known as les cépages nobles.

Any of these 'noble grapes' may be left to ripen on the vines beyond the normal picking time if the autumn is a fine one. When greater concentrations of sugar have been achieved by this extra ripening, late harvest wines, known as vendanges tardives, are produced. If the so-called 'noble rot' (pourriture noble), caused by the benign fungus botrytis cinerea, develops, then glycerol is produced as well as the aromas and flavours being changed and enhanced. These grapes produce luscious dessert wines, known as séléction de grains nobles.

Another very individual grape planted in Alsace is the Muscat. It makes a lovely aperitif. It is also recommended by local people as a perfect accompaniment to asparagus, which is cultivated extensively here, and which is notoriously difficult to partner with wine. The problem for the consumer is that the name sounds confusingly like Muscadet, or Muscat Beaumes de Venise. In fact, Muscat d'Alsace is a bone-dry wine which is piercingly fruity, one of the grapiest of all wines. Smell it once and you will always recognise it, for it is just like the best hothouse Muscat dessert grapes - despite being dry, which is rather puzzling! The fact that sweetness and fruitiness are two different things is often demonstrated in Alsace.

In addition, the Pinot Blanc is widely planted and gives wine which is flowery, easy to appreciate and often excellent value. Sylvaner used to be an important Alsace grape but it is losing in popularity to Pinot Blanc, perhaps because the former can sometimes be rather neutral.

The wines of Alsace suffer from something of an image problem. This may date back to the time when, after the Franco-Prussian war and the French defeat in 1870, Alsace became part of Germany and production of its finest wine diminished in favour of volume production of cheaper qualities. But Alsace returned to France in 1918 and has been rebuilding its reputation as a fine wine area ever since. It is true, however, that they have not always helped their own cause by shipping wines for export with residual sugar and high sulphur content which can cause headaches.

People often ask how to match Alsace wine with food - all too often the consumer is not very adventurous in this respect and falls back on a tried and tested combination from other regions. This is understandable as good Alsace wines are not cheap. However, the net result is that there are many fine winemakers whose quality products are mainly ignored by those who buy and consume fine wine.

Alsace wines were mainly fronted in export markets by merchant shippers, such as Hugel in Riquewihr or Trimbach in Ribeauvillé. They are both famous, fine old firms who have their own estates; they also buy in grapes to vinify at the time of the harvest and sometimes also wine made by other growers, which they then bottle. There is a growers' movement encouraged by consumer demand for authenticity - increasingly people like to be able to identify the producer and know the precise origins of the wine they are buying. There is also a strong co-operative movement and cellars like those in Turkheim are major flag-bearers for Alsace.

TRADITIONAL RECIPES AND DANCING IN THE VINES

"Vins d'Alsace. Pierre Freudenreich & Fils. De père en fils depuis 1653". A polished brass plaque in the wall, next to an archway in the charming main street of the village of Eguisheim, announces proudly that this family has been making wine here for over three hundred years. The archway leads to a flowery, galleried courtyard where a trailer of grapes is being unloaded into the vat-house Up some wooden stairs Mme Freudenreich, helped by two married daughters, is busy in the kitchen, as she has been every harvest for the last forty years.

Lunch is served punctually at mid-day in the vines. At a quarter to twelve, the food is loaded into a small jeep backed up to the foot of the stairs. Mimi, one of the Freudenreich daughters, takes the steering wheel. An elderly man climbs in beside her - an ex-bank clerk, long retired, he has been coming to do the harvest for even longer than Mme Freudenreich has been cooking. Mimi's daughter gets back from school just in time to hop in among the pots and plates in the back, and they're off.

Alsace villages are usually either Protestant or Roman Catholic, not mixed. As this one is Catholic it is not a surprise to find a large Christ on the Cross by the roadside at the corner of the vineyard where the Freudenreich's pickers are just finishing their rows. A table and benches have been set up next to it. Mimi starts laying out plates and cutlery and other members of the family arrive to help. One brings a baby who is passed from lap to lap during the meal, happily trying a taste of this and that. Vegetable soup is ladled out, turkey escalopes in breadcrumbs are kept warm to follow it, and the pickers sit down in the sunshine. Neighbours driving by with truckloads of grapes hoot and wave.

The cheese - a local Munster - is on the table. A few leaves of salad are left in the huge bowl and Mimi is encouraging people to finish them. Some, following the local habit, are eating their cheese with potatoes rather than bread. One of the pickers fetches her accordion, which has come up in the jeep, and sits on an upturned hotte (the grapes are emptied into these by the pickers when their baskets are full) to play. It quickly turns into a sing-song and one older couple get up and dance, to applause from the rest.

Among this small band of sixteen pickers many have been coming back for twelve, or in some cases fifteen or sixteen years. Their fidelity is in part to do with the food. Here they continue to cook the old-fashioned dishes of Alsace so suited to feeding hungry people working in the fields. There is red cabbage with apples, cooked slowly for two hours and served with roast pork and potatoes; choucroute garni, the Alsace version of sauerkraut - for which finely chopped cabbage is salted in a barrel so that it ferments slightly, then rinsed of salt, cooked in white wine and served with smoked bacon joints and smoked sausages; there is coq an Riesling, which is chicken cooked in local white wine and usually served with the special Alsace noodles called spaetzle. There is also the other celebrated local speciality, baeckaoffa, a mixture of pork, beef and lamb, layered with carrots and potatoes, and cooked for at least three hours. The harvest menus, here as elsewhere, also include the range of country cooking such as blanquettes, fricassés, boulettes to use up left- over meat, and a good purée rose (pink purée) made by mixing potato and carrot in a smooth mash to serve with roasts.

Included in the dessert repertoire are the classic floating islands, caramel cream, apple compôte and the local fruit tarts made with yeast pastry. No wonder pickers keep coming back here.

(Since I wrote those lines, the elderly man has, I am sorry to say, passed away, but on a happier note the little girl mentioned has qualified as a doctor. The Freudenreich family continue to feed their pickers in the same way).

Recipes from the French Wine Harvest

VENDANGES À LA CARTE IN RODERN

The harvest here in Alsace differs from most other areas in that it does not necessarily continue uninterruptedly for two or three weeks. Rather, it is a question of vendanges à la carte. It may start with several days in September, picking the Muscat grapes which ripen earliest - they need to be picked before they are over-ripe because otherwise the crisp acidity which balances the intense fruitiness is lost. In October, the later-ripening Riesling is picked. There may be a gap of three weeks before the vendanges tardives, usually in November, depending on weather conditions. Most growers find it convenient to use local people.

Mme Koehly is a formidable lady. Brought up in a family of wine-growers who also had a small merchant's business and a restaurant with rooms, she is used to hard work. She married her husband when times were tough for the Alsace vignerons and prices achieved for their wine were low. They were determined to succeed but it meant working long hours. They took no holidays. Everything they made was put back into the estate, to buy more land or to instal better equipment.

She remembers her mother making sure that the men working in the cellars got a good start to the day - there was soup, two fried eggs and a pair of Strasbourg sausages each for breakfast. At 10.00 a.m. there was a break for coffee and schnapps - it was the custom of the older people to pour some of their schnapps over a piece of bread and eat it. The real picking very often started only at 1.00 p.m. and finished at 5.00, so there was no need to provide a mid-day meal, just coffee and the inevitable schnapps at the start, 'and the old peasant women insisted on being given cigarettes,' remembers Mme Koehly. Everyone had a miniature barrel (le tonnelet) filled with something to drink to take to the vines.

Rosi Hanson

A pig was killed to provide pork dishes for the evening meals at harvest time. Joints were salted or smoked, sausages made. Boudins (black puddings) sometimes burst while they were being boiled. This was turned to good account as a soup, poured over toast.

The head, feet and lungs were all used to make a dish glorying in the name of schweinspaper. It does not sound very enticing and Mme Koehly admits that it is not much liked and hardly ever made in these more affluent days. One way of using the pig's head that has survived is called presskopf. After cooking, the skin and bones are removed, and the meat, with the tongue and ears, pressed into a mould. This is a kind of brawn, excellent when sliced and eaten cold with little gherkins, as a first course. The fillet of pork was, and still is, salted, then smoked to make kassler. This can be eaten cold, rather like raw ham, or roasted and eaten as a hot joint.

The Koehlys succeeded in building up an excellent estate in and around Rodern and handed over to their son, Christian. He is part of the growers' movement, energetically promoting the fine wines of Alsace at home and abroad, hoping to persuade gourmets everywhere to experiment by partnering meat dishes of all kinds with these wines, just as they do here.

CASSEROLE OF RED CABBAGE & APPLES
Chou Rouge aux Pommes

FOR 6 PEOPLE
1 red cabbage, weighing about 1 kg (2 lb)
1 tablespoon sunflower or groundnut oil
2-3 tablespoons red wine vinegar
2-3 medium-size eating apples
salt and pepper

Cut the tough outside leaves off the cabbage. Cut it in four and cut out the hard white stalk. Now slice the cabbage finely.

Heat the oil in a large heavy-based pan and toss the cabbage in it for about 5 minutes. Stir in the vinegar. Peel, core and slice the apples. Add to the cabbage, mixing them together. Add salt and pepper, and water almost to the top of the cabbage. Bring to simmering point, cover and cook, either on top or in a medium-slow oven for two hours.

A variation can be made using fresh or vacuum-packed chestnuts instead of apples: 20 - 25 (peeled, if fresh) should be added to the cabbage.

Both versions are nice with roast pork or pork chops.

TRADITIONAL PICKLED CABBAGE WITH SMOKED PORK AND SAUSAGES
Choucroute Garni

In the old days, families made their own choucroute, but now it is usually bought ready-prepared from a charcuterie, which also sells the sausages and pork joints to go with it.

The first step is to track down a source of good choucroute (of course you can get it in tins), as well as smoked boiling sausages, such as Strasbourg or the similar Frankfurter sausages, and the salted and smoked pork joints needed. A jambonneau (hock and hand), a neat little ham, is often used, and sometimes carré salé (salted fore loin in a piece). If no salted pork is available you might consider using some fried pork chops, or roasting a piece of loin of pork or adding some different sausages.

FOR 6 PEOPLE
1.5 kg (3 lb) choucroute
2 medium onions
125 g (4 oz) goose fat or butter
1 large glass of Riesling
250 ml (8 fl oz) stock (chicken stock would be suitable - if no stock is available use water and increase the amount of wine)
1 bay leaf
1 clove garlic
10 juniper berries
6 coriander seeds
salt and pepper

FOR THE GARNISH:
750g (1½ lb) salted loin of pork
500 - 625 g (1 - 1¼ lb) smoked bacon in a piece
6 medium potatoes, peeled
a jambonneau (see above), if available
6 Strasbourg or Frankfurter sausages
1 small glass of kirsch or other eau de vie, optional

'Wash the choucroute in cold water once or twice depending on the season,' it says rather quaintly in a traditional recipe. This is because a large quantity of choucroute would be made to last the whole winter - by the end of winter it was likely to be fermenting in the barrel and needed washing very thoroughly.

Drain the choucroute, pressing it to squeeze out the moisture. Peel and chop the onions finely, then fry them in the goose fat or butter in a flameproof casserole large enough to hold all the meat. Before the onions brown, add the choucroute, tossing it in the fat with a wooden fork for about 15 minutes. Add the glass of wine and some of the stock or water - just enough to moisten it all without the choucroute floating in it. Add the bay leaf, garlic, juniper, coriander seeds, salt and pepper. Cover and simmer for about an hour. Stir the choucroute and check that it has enough stock, then add the salted pork, if you have it, and the smoked bacon joint to the casserole and cook for another hour. Now put the peeled whole potatoes to cook on top of the choucroute for a further half hour. Boil a pan of water to simmer the jambonneau, if you have it, and the Strasbourg or Frankfurter sausages for 20 minutes.

Some people add a small glass of kirsch, or one of the other eaux de vie liked so much in Alsace, to the choucroute just before serving. Pile the choucroute up on a dish, arrange slices of the pork joints and the sausages on top and potatoes round the edges. Serve with mustard.

Recipes from the French Wine Harvest

PINK PURÉE
Purée Rose

This purée is excellent with roasts. You need equal quantities of peeled potatoes and carrots plus butter, milk and seasoning.

Cook the vegetables in salted water, drain and purée. Season and beat in butter and a little warmed milk until you reach the desired smooth, creamy texture. It is a very pretty colour.

Other root vegetables can be added. Turnips and/or celeriac are particularly good. The purée can be made in advance and warmed in a bowl over a pan of simmering water when needed.

CHICKEN POACHED IN RIESLING WITH CREAM SAUCE
Coq au Riesling

This is the version used by the Freudenreichs. They serve it with Spaetzle, the Alsace noodles (see below). Use a free-range chicken. Cut it up into 8 portions, or buy chicken joints such as legs (drumstick and thigh attached).

FOR 4 - 6 PEOPLE
1 chicken, weighing about 1.5 kg (3 lb), jointed
60 g (2 oz) butter

1 tablespoon oil
4 shallots
1 clove garlic
1 small glass cognac
500 ml (15 fl oz) Riesling
sprig parsley and bay leaf
salt, pepper and grated nutmeg
400 ml (14 fl oz) crème fraîche

Brown the chicken pieces in a mixture of butter and oil in a flameproof casserole. Put aside. Peel the shallots and garlic and chop finely. Add them to the butter mixture and let them take colour. Put the chicken pieces back. Warm the cognac in a small pan. Pour it over the chicken and, standing back, ignite carefully. When the flames die down, add the Riesling just to cover and the herbs. Bring to simmering point, cover and leave to cook gently for 30 to 45 minutes, until the chicken pieces are tender.

When they are cooked, lift them out and keep them warm. Taste the broth. You could now choose to reduce it by fast boiling for 5 to 10 minutes in order to give it a depth of flavour. If you take this step, add the seasoning afterwards, having tasted again.

Stir in some of the crème fraîche and perhaps a little butter. Taste and add more cream until you feel it is right. Sieve the sauce, pour over the chicken and serve.

ALSACE NOODLES
Spaetzle

Mimi (or rather, Marie-Léonce) Ling-Freudenreich constantly wins prizes for her Coq au Riesling and Spaetzles- these things are taken seriously here. This is her recipe. It is enough to accompany one chicken cooked in Riesling. It may sound a little daunting, but is well worth trying.

FOR 6 PEOPLE
8 eggs
salt
grated nutmeg
500 (1 lb)flour
2 tablespoons fine semolina
100 ml (3½ fl oz) water
1 tablespoon sunflower or groundnut oil
30 g (1 oz) butter

Break the eggs in a big bowl. Beat them as though for an omelette. Add salt and a little nutmeg.

Stir in the flour and the semolina little by little, working into the eggs carefully. When they are incorporated, add the glass of water and stir it in. Aim for a consistency between a batter and a dough. Leave to rest for at least an hour.

Get ready a large pan of water. Add salt and a spoonful of oil and bring to the boil. Pour, or press, the flour mixture through a colander with large holes (it needs to be one without a foot - there is a special implement for the purpose but you can improvise) into the hot water. As it goes through the holes into the hot water, it turns into worm-like, or tadpole-like, pasta. Like gnocchi, the noodles are cooked when they rise to the top of the pan. Lift them out with a slotted spoon and plunge them into a large bowl of cold water - the water stops them going dry and they swell a little.When all the noodles have been cooked and cooled, drain them, then sauté them in butter until slightly crisp, in a frying-pan.

Rosi Hanson

FRENCH HOT-POT – A CASSEROLE OF SLOW COOKED BEEF, PORK AND LAMB AND POTATOES
Baeckaoffa/ Potée Boulangère

Tradition has it that this dish was made on washing day. Housewives took their casseroles to the baker's oven (hence its name) to cook during the day while they got on with the weekly wash.

There is an oval, glazed, earthenware casserole with lid which is made specially for this in Alsace, but any casserole which has the sort of lid that you can seal with a flour and water paste will be suitable. But perhaps, even better, you could just substitute tin foil for the paste.

FOR 8 PEOPLE
500 g (1 lb) stewing beef
500 g (1 lb) shoulder or leg of pork, boned
500 g (1 lb) shoulder of lamb, boned
1 kg (2 lb) potatoes
500 g (1 lb) carrots
butter for greasing
flour and water for the seal

FOR THE MARINADE:
4 shallots
2 onions
2 cloves garlic

1-2 carrots
bouquet garni
salt and pepper
approximately 500 ml (15fl oz) Riesling

Cut up the meat into cubes. Put all the meat into a bowl with the marinade vegetables, peeled and chopped, the bouquet garni, salt, pepper and the wine. Marinate overnight.

Preheat the oven to gas mark 6, 400°F, 200°C.

Peel the potatoes and carrots and slice quite thickly. Butter the casserole. Put in alternate layers of potatoes, carrots and the different meats, seasoning as you go, until you reach the top. You can include the chopped onions, etc. from the marinade if you like. The final layer should be potato.

Pour in the wine from the marinade. It should reach about half-way up the casserole - add more if necessary.
Put on the lid. Mix some flour and water to a sticky paste to seal the lid in place, or use tin foil.

Bake in the preheated oven for approximately three hours, turning the heat down after the first hour to gas mark 3, 325°F, 160°C.

Break the flour seal carefully so that the bits do not fall into the dish. Serve the baeckaoffa with a green salad - anything else would be too heavy.

USEFUL YEAST PASTRY FOR TARTS IN THE ALSACE MANNER
Pâte Levée Briochée

This recipe is the one given in a small local French publication, 'Petit Recueil de la Gastronomie Alsacienne'. It can be used as a savoury or sweet tart base.

FOR 4 - 6 PEOPLE
10 g (¼ oz) dried yeast (not 'easy-blend')
100 ml (3½ fl oz) warm milk
250 g (8 oz) plain flour
1 pinch of salt
40 g (1¼ oz) sugar
60 g (2 oz) butter, softened
2 egg whites

Mix the yeast with a little of the warm milk. Put 60 g (2 oz) of the flour in a bowl and make a well into which you put the yeast. Mix together to make a soft starter dough. Cover it with a clean cloth and leave it somewhere warm, not hot, until it doubles in volume (depending on the ambient temperature and humidity, this could take about an hour).

Put the rest of the flour in a bowl. In the middle of it put the salt, sugar, warm milk and the softened butter. Mix all these ingredients, add the egg whites, then the starter dough. Knead by hand until you can see air bubbles and the dough comes away from the side of the bowl. Leave, covered, in a warm place, until it doubles in size, probably between 1 and 2 hours.

When the dough has risen, knead it again for a few minutes, adding a little flour if it is sticky. If you are using it as the base for the plum tart, spread it over an oiled tart tin or baking sheet, arrange the fruit on top, then proceed as described in recipe below.

PLUM TART
Tarte aux Quetschs

Recipes from the French Wine Harvest

This open plum tart can use the yeast pastry as above or pâte sablée, a crumbly sweet pastry. These local plums are large, oval and dark-skinned: the sort that are used for drying and for cooking, known as Quetsch or Quetsche. They are in season in September, when these tarts are much eaten. Quetschs can be sharp-tasting and therefore will need plenty of sugar. Otherwise, use whatever plums are available and adjust the sugar according to their natural sweetness.

FOR 4 - 6 PEOPLE
For the pastry to line a 20 cm (8 in) tart tin
(usually with a removable-base and fluted-edges):
pinch of salt
3 teaspoons white caster sugar
175 g (6 oz) plain flour, sieved
90 g (3 oz) butter at room temperature
4 tablespoons iced water

FOR THE FILLING:
1 kg (2 lb) ripe plums
30 - 60 g (1 - 2 oz) caster sugar
a little powdered cinnamon
icing sugar

Preheat the oven to gas mark 6, 400°F, 200°C. Put a heavy baking sheet in the middle.

Grease a 20 cm (8 in) tart tin with butter. Add the salt and sugar to the flour in a mixing bowl. Rub the butter into the flour. Add about half the water to moisten - adding more if it seems necessary - the pastry should be crumbly, not sticky and wet. Straightaway make it into a ball and put it into the middle of the buttered tart tin. Use your hands to press it down, spreading it over the base of the tin and gradually up round the edges. Trim off any extra round the edges.

Halve or quarter the plums (depending on size) and take out the stones. Arrange them on the pastry, in concentric circles. The fruit shrinks as it cooks, so it needs to be closely packed. Sprinkle with the sugar and cinnamon. Bake on top of the baking sheet in the preheated oven for 30 to 40 minutes.
When the tart is cooked, slide it out of the tin and onto a cooling rack. It can be served warm or cold with a little icing sugar sprinkled over it.

Rosi Hanson

There is an interesting local custom - the tart is made using pâte levée briochée (in other words the yeast-raised pastry) with a more cake-like texture, and accompanies a thick homemade vegetable soup. This is not so strange as it might at first seem when it is remembered how many savoury dishes contain prunes. David Ling, the English Export Director of the wine-merchants Hugel et Fils, in Riquewihr is a convert to this gastronomic curiosity. 'It sounds revolting, but I can assure you, from at-first-reluctant personal experience, it is delicious, and the combination of flavours is phenomenal!

BIBLIOGRAPHY

Adventures on the Wine Route, by Kermit Lynch, published Farrar, Straus & Giroux
Charcuterie and French Pork Cookery, by Jane Grigson, published Penguin
Cooking with de Pomiane, by Edouard de Pomiane, published Faber & Faber
Cooking with Wine, by Robin McDouall, published Penguin
Ethnocuisine de la Bourgogne, by A. Sloimovich, published Cormarin
French Country Cooking, by Elizabeth David, published Penguin
French Provincial Cooking, by Elizabeth David, published Penguin
La Cuisine de France, by Mapie, the Countess de Toulouse-Lautrec, published Orion
La Cuisinière Provençale, by J.-B. Reboul, published Tacussel
Larousse Gastronomique, published Hamlyn
Lulu's Provençal Table, by Richard Olney, published HarperCollins.
Mastering the Art of French Cooking, Vols 1 & 2, by Simone Beck, Louisette Bertholle, Julia Child, published Penguin
Mediterranean Seafood, by Alan Davidson, published Penguin
Modern French Culinary Art, by Henri Paul Pellaprat, published World
On Food and Cooking, the Science and Lore of the Kitchen, by Harold McGee, published George Allen and Unwin Ltd
Petit Recueil de la Gastronomie Alsacienne, by Marguerite Doerflinger, published Editions SAEP
Recettes en Provence, by André Maureau, published Edisud.
Simple French Food, by Richard Olney, published Jill Norman & Hobhouse Ltd
The Escoffier Cook Book, published Crown

ACKNOWLEDGEMENTS

I am particularly grateful to all the wine-making families described in the text. On many occasions I met several generations who generously gave their recipes, anecdotes and culinary tips, hospitably opening bottles and inviting me to share meals.

I would especially like to thank those who allowed me to hang about their harvest kitchens, asking questions, when they were at their busiest and those who made it possible for us to photograph work in the vines, vat-houses and kitchens at such a nerve-racking time.
During several harvests I had many conversations with pickers and I am grateful to all those who took the time to share their experiences.

Many other people contributed either by giving contacts or background information. In particular, my grateful thanks go to Gerald Asher, the late Madame Simon Bize, Charles and Marie-France Blagdon, William and Trudy Bolter, Michel Cestia, Mme Serge Dagueneau, Cathie Faller, the Franquet-Monthelon family, Gillian Mawrey, Christian Moueix, Mme Henri Richou, Patrick and Sachiko Saulnier Blache and Peter Wasserman.

I would like to thank Sandy McArthur for her help during a research trip to the Loire and Katrina Erskine and James Anderson for their help and hospitality during a trip to the Rhône. Becky Wasserman and Russell Hone were most generous, kindly allowing us to cook recipes and photograph them in their Bouilland home, as well as giving much useful information and encouragement.

Many friends were stalwart in testing and re-testing recipes: particular thanks to Ken Blakely, Jonathan Courage, Elizabeth Shirreff, Augusta Skidelsky, Paul Wasserman, Lyn Fry, Daisy MacDonald.

Thanks go to Rosemary Wilkinson for believing in the original idea and for her help in bringing the first edition of the book to completion; to Jay Hornsby for expert editing of that edition, and to photographer Katerina Kalogeraki for her patience and skill, working in taxing conditions on both editions.

I am forever grateful to George Berg and Andy Berg for technical help, and to Tony Orsi & the team at Netro42.

I also thank my son, Christopher Hanson for technical expertise, and for eating and making constructive comments on all the recipes.

Finally, I owe the greatest debt of thanks to my husband, Anthony Hanson MW. I have been able to draw on his many years' experience of wine-trading and, as ever, he has been more than generous in sharing his knowledge. Without him I would never have met the growers, picked the harvests, drunk the wines or eaten the food that inspired the book.

BIOGRAPHY

As a young writer Rosi Hanson lived and worked in Burgundy where she wrote a column for a local paper about her experiences, and picked two harvests.

Bitten by the food and wine bug, she then spent two years working for the cookery writer Elizabeth David at her legendary kitchen equipment shop in London.

She wrote Recipes from the French Wine Harvest, first published in 1995, a book which took her into the kitchens and cellars of many of the greatest chateaux and domaines in the six main wine regions of France.

She is a regular contributor to Decanter and to Langtons on-line magazine in Australia.

She is married to a Master of Wine, and lives in London and Paris.

Printed in Great Britain
by Amazon.co.uk, Ltd.,
Marston Gate.